The Mini-Society

The Mini-Society Workbook
Everything You Need to Create a
Mini-Society in Your Classroom

Kathleen D. Fletcher

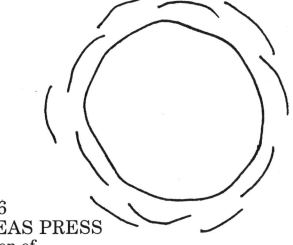

1996
TEACHER IDEAS PRESS
A Division of
Libraries Unlimited, Inc.
Englewood, Colorado

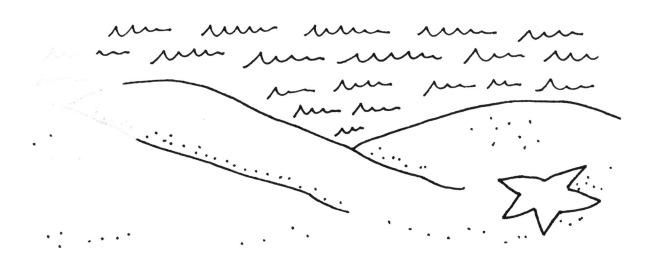

*In loving memory of my precious mom. I shall miss
her enthusiasm and involvement in
my societies and Mini-Faires.*

TEACHER IDEAS PRESS
A Division of
Libraries Unlimited, Inc.
P.O. Box 6633
Englewood, CO 80155-6633
1-800-237-6124

Louisa M. Griffin, *Production Editor*
Constance Hardesty, *Copy Editor*
Tama J. Serfoss, *Proofreader*
Pamela J. Getchell, *Layout and Design*

Library of Congress Cataloging-in-Publication Data

Fletcher, Kathleen D.
    The mini-society workbook : everything you need to create a mini-
society in your classroom / Kathleen D. Fletcher.
    xi, 149 p. 22x28 cm.
    ISBN 1-56308-347-7
    1. Social sciences--Study and teaching (Elementary)--United
States--Handbooks, manuals, etc. 2. Group work in education--United
States--Handbooks, manuals, etc. 3. Interdisciplinary approach in
education--United States--Handbooks, manuals, etc. 4. Classroom
management--United States--Handbooks, manuals, etc. I. Title.
LB1584.F54   1995
372.83--dc20
                                                            95-14430
                                                            CIP

Contents

Acknowledgments

Special thanks are made to my husband and three daughters for their patience and encouragement during my preoccupation; to my dad, a fellow teacher, for his invaluable time in helping me prepare the first version of this book; to my sister for her contribution to my work during the early stages of writing; and to all parents and teachers who supported my Mini-Society program, especially Nancy Strinz and Barbara Stuehrmann.

This book is dedicated to Jim Harris, the teacher who inspired me to create my first Mini-Society and develop this program; to the fantastic students of Great Britain, Russia, Cryton, Antsodea, Tropical Island, Astara, the Land of the Money Munchers, Hammertown, Ocean's End, Castle Rock, and Lost Lagoon—thanks for your enthusiasm, creativity, and love of your society in our classroom; to Dianne Jorgensen and Cora Jacobson, two secretaries who supported all my crazy requests; and to Roger Klinkhart, a principal who was a real trooper during all of our reenactments.

Introduction

What is a Mini-Society? A Mini-Society is exactly what the name implies: a "mini" society. Within the classroom, it is the creation of a new world (society) for the duration of the school year. A Mini-Society is an experience-based economics education program. It is also a classroom management program that integrates curricula in an interdisciplinary approach.

Why Create a Mini-Society?

Why should a Mini-Society be integrated into your classroom? I can explain this by giving an example: Social studies is not one of my favorite subjects to teach. Yes, teaching all the interesting and fascinating facts is fun; however, being consistently faced with the fact that students will not remember most of this information is frustrating, no matter how exciting the material is. It is difficult for many students to relate to the abstractness that characterizes textbook learning.

This dilemma led me to question how I could make social studies real and meaningful to students' daily lives. How could I ensure their retention of the concepts beyond the year that I had them in class? How could I inspire them to relate to the historical significance of, for example, how their own state developed, the evolution of the United States, or the importance of different cultures around the world?

I began reenacting history itself with a fellow colleague (we were Great Britain, the students were the colonies). I immediately noticed a change in their learning and motivation levels. Following our "Revolutionary War" (see appendix A), I knew my dilemma had a solution. The physical reenactment of the social studies lesson caused this historical event to become more real to the students. And that is how the Mini-Society program was born and this workbook developed.

The Mini-Society Workbook provides the necessary tools to reap the benefits of an enriched social studies curriculum that also integrates multiple subject areas. Take it step-by-step and you too will experience the successes I've enjoyed in helping my students to learn, plus a few added benefits: Class unity and pride, respect for each other and the classroom, more creative thinking, increased self-esteem, the learning of life skills, developing responsibility, increased enthusiasm, the involvement of parents, the ability to reach a broad spectrum of children and bring to the surface their individual abilities and strengths, and better management of the classroom with a positive environment.

Integrating the Mini-Society into Your Curriculum

You will find that the creation of a Mini-Society is a strong interdisciplinary approach that easily integrates your existing social studies curriculum. Using your current textbook, carefully prioritize the major concepts you want to teach. For example, the early history of your state or the 13 colonies' quest for independence from England. Interweave this curriculum with the Mini-Society curriculum. You are creating a real-life society in your classroom that incorporates the historical events discussed in your textbook. My first two societies were modeled after Great Britain and Russia and led to my creation of the Mini-Society concept. Here are some ideas for grades 3 through 9:

Third grade. While learning about communities, create your own in the classroom.

Fourth grade. In conjunction with your curriculum, model your society after a state you study or create a new state. (It is important for students to learn everything they can about their state to create their society.)

Fifth grade. Model the beginnings of your society after the colonies as you teach the early history of the United States. Evolve the "colony" society into a "state" society. (See the classroom example of the colony of Hammertown in appendix A.)

Sixth grade. While teaching about various world societies, compare them to your own classroom society.

Seventh through ninth grades. Integrate the principles of government into your classroom society.

A Mini-Society can integrate more than just social studies. It can integrate language arts, mathematics, fine arts, computer technology, industry, economics, government, creative writing, the uses of multimedia expression, and serve as a foundation for classroom management.

A Teacher's Responsibilities

For the first two months, you will help begin the society. You'll be taking the class through Phase I and Phase II. A word of caution: Do not try to mold or control the shape of the society. Let the students make the decisions and assume ownership. You are the facilitator, the key that turns the ignition. The students are the fuel! By Phase III, you can become a private citizen, a government official, a businessperson, or whatever!

Although my students were the creators and managers of their societies, each needed the security of a figurehead. I was still the teacher. I have found that students lack the experience and maturity to handle power over one another and, therefore, need a figurehead. (This, I'm sure, is the reason why my classes' societies have named me Supreme Being, Emperor, Queen, and Admiral, among others.)

Your role in the Mini-Society should be similar to your role with any classroom curriculum: to guide students toward discovering the concepts for themselves. That's when learning takes on meaning.

Time Management

Each step in Phases I and II will take approximately 20 to 30 minutes. The remaining phases will require only 35 minutes once a week. The ongoing society activities will be absorbed by your classroom curriculum. Because the early weeks of September lend themselves to extra time before all your subject curriculum is started, you can usually (and will want to) finish Phase I by October. Here's a typical schedule:

September to October: Complete Phase I. Begin Phase II.

October to November: Complete Phase II. Begin Phase III.

November to June: Complete Phase III and carry out Phases IV, V, and VI during the ensuing months.

So, without further ado, let's get this show on the road!

Phase I
Creating the Environment

In the first phase of creating a Mini-Society in your classroom, the main emphasis will be on the development of the atmosphere or environment of the new society.

To create the environment, students will need to name their society, name the inhabitants (by gender), design the currency, develop cooperative learning teams, select society colors, adopt a flag and its pledge, design a street map for addresses, and creatively add other unique trademarks or symbols as they are inspired. You will be responsible for informing the students' parents about the program and keeping things moving toward the development of the environment.

If, after Phase I, your society sends me a birth announcement, I will respond. Societies also can communicate with me via modem. Write to: Kathleen Fletcher, 611 N. Vista Bonita, Glendora, CA 91741; or send e-mail to Fredmail address: KFletcher@chtroak.cerf.fred.org or to Internet address: fletcher.apu.edu.

Step 1
Name the Society

The first time you create a Mini-Society, you need to prepare the students. They will not have any idea what a Mini-Society is. Explain that you are creating a brand new world/society in your classroom. The successive years will be easier. Experience generates confidence. Kids share with other kids, and word gets out that you create Mini-Societies in your classroom. Students will actually come to your classroom anticipating the Mini-Society.

The first and most important step in the process of creating a new society is naming it. The society's name greatly influences the direction your society will take. The name can't be something that already exists, such as Narnia, or the name of a toy, like Construx. It must be made up. It is nice if the name can fit around a theme. For example, when my class was Lost Lagoon, it was easy to decorate the room like a lagoon and find "Gilligan's Island" type of things to go with it.

Let students think of names as a homework assignment and bring their ideas to class the next day. They may submit as many ideas as they wish. I ask them to put their names on their papers so I can acknowledge the student who created the name after the selection. Initially, it is best to leave ideas anonymous so that popularity isn't a factor in the selection.

Have students write the name and it's phonetic spelling on their paper. For example:

Antsodea - Antsōdēá

Here's the best way I've found to handle the name selection process:

1. List all the names on the overhead or chalkboard. Eliminate any names that already exist.

2. Read through each name once and then as a class. It is important at this point not to let the students know whether you like or dislike certain names. Resist the temptation! I find this hard to do sometimes. You may also need to encourage the students to be courteous and to respect everyone's ideas.

3. Cut a pile of scrap paper in half to use as ballots. Each student votes for 5-10 favorites on a private ballot. You cannot vote. Remember, you are only the catalyst.

4. Tally the votes. Circle or rewrite the 5-10 favorites on the overhead or chalkboard.

5. Say the names again. Remind the students to be sure they like the name because they will be using it all year long.

6. Each student now votes for only one name. This is the final vote.

7. Tally the votes in front of all the students. This creates a lot of enthusiasm.

8. Record the date and time the society was born.

9. Put this information in a large manila envelope. It will become part of the historical archives of the society!

This procedure may sound tedious, but it's important. The name of your society will be the spinoff for lots of creative ideas throughout the school year. Here are examples of how two societies got their names:

Birth of Antsodea

Soundwave
Umpqua
Antsodea
Viking
Thundertron
Comp-u-car
Centern
Trogan
Poetry
Computron
Rainbowland
Bearland
Unicorn
Triconie
Olembie
Uni
Septmis
Conqua

Antsodea
Thundertron
Comp-u-cor
Computron

11:24 A.M.
9/20/85
Antsodea
was born

Weekend Busters

Paraexcellence
Perelandia
Panasia II
Bronchitus I
Polyites
Landora III
Eduville
Soteach
Ceres I
Asterburg
Creatives I
Spotlights I
Mania
Manic
(Weekend Busters) IIII II
Atlantic I
Utopia I
Dragonland

7:00 P.M.
8/8/86
Weekend
Busters
was born

Step 2
Announcing the Society

You now have a unique name and need to make it official to the rest of the world. Create an announcement to place in your school's daily bulletin or monthly newsletter. Let the students help you be creative. Have fun with it!

Sample announcements:

On Friday, Sept. 11, 1992, at 11:03 a.m., L-2 invented a time machine that accidentally took them back to the middle ages where they discovered **Castle Rock**. The time machine broke, so the knights and damsels are stuck there! The drawbridge operator is very chivalrous though, so come visit us!

* *

After a smashing shipwreck on Friday, Sept. 6, 1991, the brave colonists swam ashore and founded a new colony named **Ocean's End**. The Pirates and Piratettes of L-2, along with Captain Fletcher, are in the process of building their colony. Their currency is called Coral Cash if you need to do some trading.

* *

For those of you who survived the earthquake yesterday, California has a new island off its coast. H-3 is now known as **Tropical Island**, born on September 14, 1987, at 2:26 p.m.

Mrs. Fletcher, the Queen

If you are the first to create a Mini-Society at your school, you may receive some funny reactions. The last sample announcement generated the following response: "I didn't know we had an earthquake yesterday. I didn't even feel it!"

Birth announcements are also fun to do. You can send them to other societies, parents, or me. Remember to save a copy of all you do for your historical archives! See the following three examples.

Her Royal Majesty Queen Kathleen
> *Queen of Scots*
> *Queen of Wales*
> *Queen of Northern Ireland*
> *Queen of England*
> *Queen of Commonwealth*
and her Royal Prime Minister Martha,

We announce the birth of a Nation:
> *ATLANTIS*

As yet we still have a priminive society with no economy or government—except for a chief. How about a little foreign aid? We are starving—we just had a drought and the enemy is coming!

Chief Harris

This is a reproduction of the first birth announcement that was sent to our society. It was written on a piece of paper bag!

Announcing the birth of

ASTARA

(A new planet in our galaxy!)

Born on September 9th, 1988 at 9:33 a.m.

On Friday, September 10, the L-2 Titanic went on a 3 hour tour. The weather started getting rough. The tiny ship was tossed. If not for the courage of the fearless crew from Cedargrove, they would not have found their new home at 10:26 a.m....

The Lost Lagoon

S.O.S.
Admiral Fletcher
Skipper Nieto
Sea Serpents &
Flamingos

Send note in glass bottle

Step 3
Name the Inhabitants

All my societies have wanted special words to mean *boys* and *girls*. In one Mini-Society, Cryton, each student had a special name. That's okay. Let students be as creative as they like. The naming process is identical to naming the society (Step 1), except I have found it better to let the girls name the girls and the boys name the boys. (They should not vote for each others' names.) Encourage the students to think of names that go with the name of the society and with each other.

Most of my societies have wanted to give titles to me and other people that work in the room on a regular basis. The office staff may get in on the action too!

Here are some examples:

Society	Boys	Girls	Teacher
Cryton	Pantors	Miglets	Emperor
Antsodea	Fizzers	Bubblets	
Tropical Island	Surfers	Surfettes	Queen
Astara	Androids	Asteroids	Commander
Land of the Money Munchers	Money Dudes	Munchettes	Royal Highness
Hammertown	Road Warriors	Chiselettes	Master Architect
Castle Rock	Knights	Damsels	Queen II
Ocean's End	Pirates	Piratettes	Captain
Lost Lagoon	Sea Serpents	Flamingos	Admiral

Step 4
Name the Currency

Selecting a name for the currency can be done in a class brainstorming session. Prompt students to come up with ideas that fit in with the name of the society. Write their suggestions so everyone can see them. Promote teamwork by encouraging the students to respect each other's ideas. Take a vote.

Here are some examples:

Society	Name of Currency
Cryton	Tears
Antsodea	Sodas
Tropical Island	Shells
Astara	Starbars
Land of the Money Munchers	Gold Nuggets
Hammertown	Bolts
Castle Rock	Royal Rubies
Ocean's End	Coral Cash
Lost Lagoon	Sandollars

At this point, refrain from giving ideas from past societies. I'm providing these examples to help you get the idea. You want students to develop their own uniqueness and sense ownership of their society. After they have created their society, it is fun to share the history of past societies. We have "archeological digs," where I bring in archives from previous societies and the students see how much they can discover about those societies. They really enjoy this.

You can use traditional denominations or have the class vote on what denominations they would like to have.

Step 5
Design the Money

Have each student create a design for the money as homework or an in-class art project. Students should draw one sample of each denomination with a pencil or black pen. Do not let them use colored pencil or crayons, because this design will be photocopied. Make sure students include the name of the society and the denomination in each design. The student's name should be written on the back. Have them use the worksheet on the next page.

Although students may want to make strange shapes, I have found it much easier to use rectangles. If the issue is brought up, discuss the pros and cons of other shapes with the class beforehand, for example, ease of handling, durability, and so forth.

After the designs are completed, assign a number to each and post all of them on a bulletin board or lay them on a table. Using secret ballots, have students vote for three of the designs and place their ballots in a box. I suggest voting for three because sometimes each student will vote for his or her own design, and you will have no winner!

Announce the winner after votes are tallied. The student who designed the money will make a black line master of each denomination for copying. Have them make a whole page of each denomination. Don't forget, the artist needs to be paid with the society's money for the copyright privilege of using the design.

Samples of money that have been designed are shown above.

Have students design samples of their society's money, using the forms on p. 11. Have them include various denominations. Make sure that they include their society's name and denomination on each design. Have them write their name on the back of their design.

Step 6
Develop Cooperative Learning Groups

If you use cooperative learning groups, don't forget to incorporate them into the development and problem-solving process of the society. In many situations, discussions and group projects are more effective in smaller groups. For example, I have found that writing the pledge for the flag (step 10) is more successful in groups. Let the groups select names that go with the society. They can create signs and slogans to generate team unity and enthusiasm.

Here are some examples:

<u>Ocean End's Groups</u>

Stingrays
Paradise
Surfers
Sandcrabs
Electric Eels
Sandollars

<u>Astara's Groups</u>

Mood Beamers
Shooting Stars
Space Busters

<u>Tropical Island's Groups</u>

Kiwi Seeds
Banana Peels
Coconut Shreds
Pineapple Juicers

Step 7
Inform Parents

Meet the Teacher Night is an excellent time to educate your students' parents about the Mini-Society program.

Provide a letter like the one on page 14 for parents to keep as a reference.

The most important concept you can emphasize is that when their child opens his or her business (phase 3), parents must refrain from giving the students a product to sell. The children need to work for the products.

Encourage parents to get involved. Let them know when you will have business days and auctions so they can visit.

I have had parents start their own businesses in the classroom. I also have had office staff get in on the action and open businesses. Watch out for them—they love to charge for everything. For example, they might charge students to use the phone or ask questions. It's great!

Enthusiasm soars when more people get involved. It's true, the more the merrier!

Dear Parents:

The purpose of this letter is to tell you a little about our social studies program. As you may have already heard, our time machine malfunctioned and we discovered ourselves in **CASTLE ROCK**. I'm sure your kids have filled you in on knights, damsels, and Royal Rubies! This is just the beginning of the development of a Mini-Society in our room. This activity is an economic, experience-based education program.

Students will establish their own society, print their own money, keep track of their earnings through ledgers or checkbooks, open their own businesses, and live with the consequences of their own actions within the society.

Your child may enter bank transactions; keep business records; write advertisements; produce commercials; or become a newspaper reporter, auction official, or entrepreneur. There is a lot of potential for understanding scarcity, quality control, product competition, management of finances, supply and demand, and many other concepts and life skills.

In addition to this, a unique spirit of teamwork, enthusiasm, and pride will develop in the classroom. The children will work actively in problem solving, trying to find creative and workable solutions to the numerous problems that occur in any society.

The regular social studies curriculum will be incorporated into our learning. We all know a lot can be learned from our ancestors!

You can be of great help in this program by not allowing your child to use anything for the Mini-Society from home without some sort of payment. Your child can pay by barter, our Mini-Society's currency, or an allowance. Encourage your child to think in terms of creating products or providing services to sell. Your active interest and involvement will enhance your child's learning.

I'm excited!!

Queen Fletcher II

Step 8
Select the Colors

The society is now ready to select colors that will be used in the flag, to decorate the room, and so forth. Students can suggest combinations of two colors or you can display various shades of construction paper. I staple together samples of different color combinations for students to view.

It's important that the colors are easy to find in crayons, markers, or construction paper.

Select favorite combinations and post samples on a bulletin board or list the colors on the board. Use secret ballots or a show of hands for the voting process.

Here are some colors my societies have chosen:

Cryton—blue and silver

Antsodea—burgundy and gray

Tropical Island—turquoise and gray

Astara—pink and black

We enjoy dressing in our society's colors and creating art projects around them.

Don't forget to record the date and time of any new development for the Mini-Society's historical archives. You can use the archive to make a timeline of your society to compare with your curriculum timeline.

Step 9
Adopt the Flag

Students can work individually or in cooperative learning groups to create a flag that will represent the society. I found it most effective to assign designing the flag as a homework project. Allow plenty of time for creativity and quality. Usually a week is sufficient.

The initial design can be made on an 8½" x 11" piece of white paper using colored pencils or markers. Students should write their names on the back.

Assign a number to each flag, and display all of them for voting. Students vote on secret ballots for their favorite three flags. After the field is narrowed to three choices, students vote for one flag.

When a flag has been adopted, a temporary copy needs to be made on 9" x 12" construction paper. An official 25" x 38" flag can be assembled later. Making the official flag should be a class or small group art project. You may have a parent sew the flag for you, but I find it more meaningful if it is produced by students. Spray the flag with a protector like Scotch Guard.

Each year I order an extra flag holder so that the flags from the current and all the past Mini-Societies can be displayed in the classroom. The current Mini-Society's flag should have a special place next to the United States flag or near your society's display.

As you create societies year after year, you will see history evolve, even in your flags. My first flags were felt with the designs glued on. That was before I discovered little cloth-eating bugs love that glue!

New materials are always being produced, and my flags have progressed from felt to varieties of cloth, windbreaker fabric, shiny materials, and even a beach towel. We selected fabrics that fit in with the society. The windbreaker flag was for Ocean's End, the towel was for Lost Lagoon. When puffy paints came out, we had the first puffy-paint flag! Students will notice a change from the older society flags to the newer. It's just like styles of clothes and cars! Each flag is unique.

A word of advice: Don't show flags from past Mini-Societies until the current society has completed their flag. You don't want to influence your present society's development. Also, knowing they will get to see past Mini-Societies' flags motivates students to finish their society's flag. My students, past and present, always know they can come to open house to see their flag flying.

Prepare a "fact" sheet to display with the flags. This sheet lists the historical information about the society. Include the name, date of origin, names of inhabitants, name of money, and the pledge or song.

Now you have a mini-museum of ancient flags and historical facts!

Some examples of Mini-Society flags.

Step 10
Write the Pledge

Writing the pledge can be difficult. I found when I had each student write a pledge, I'd get about one good line for every three pledges! One year we tried to combine all our favorite lines and vote. It took hours to adopt that pledge! So . . . my suggestion is that you allow students to think about it overnight, come ready with some ideas, and work in their groups on the pledge.

The pledge can be in the form of a saying, song, rap song, or cheer. Emphasize that the pledge will encompass the whole class and society.

Have each group write a pledge and present it to the rest of the class. Students vote on their favorite pledge.

The pledge can be typed, copied, and distributed to each student for memorization. Don't forget to post one copy and place one copy in the archives.

Each morning after the Pledge of Allegiance, the class will also salute their society's flag.

Some examples of pledges are:

Open your sodas, ready toast . . .
To the Bubblets and Fizzers of Antsodea who made our society come to life. We propose a toast to all the citizens of Antsodea, that we will live in justice and peace in the Antsodean way. We pledge success until the death of our land. So let's just say, CHEERS!

Jump on your surfboards, Islanders. Ready, surf . . .
We surf the waves of Tropical Island so that our waves may be totally tubular all season long. To bring truth to Tropical Island, one island, under God, till now we hold our surfboards. COW-A-BUNGA!

This pledge was a rap . . .

We're from Castle Rock and we're here to say,
We like Queen Fletcher in a major way, NOT!
We work real hard and we love to play,
Friday is when we get our pay.
We get lots of Rubies on that day, We're from Castle Rock. HOORAY, HOORAY!

This was a song to the tune of "Gilligan's Island" . . .

So . . . sit right back and you'll hear a tale, a tale of the Lost Lagoon
That started out from Cedargrove, an L-2 GATE classroom.
The admiral was a good teacher, the skipper tall and smart.
The L-2 class set sail that day for a three-hour tour, a three-hour tour.

The sea serpents took down their boat, the flamingos chomped it up.
The life raft got popped in the wreck, and they couldn't patch it up, they couldn't patch it up.

Our homework started getting rough, we felt like we were lost.
Without our Admiral Fletcher, our brains would feel like frost, our brains would feel like frost.

The ship struck ground on a shore of this uncharted Lost Lagoon
With admiral Fletcher, the skipper too, the Sea Serpents and Flamingos, some Sandollars, checks and businesses, HERE ON LOST LAGOON!

Step 11
Design a Society Map

Addresses are important for businesses and government documents. I assign each student a number. This number becomes the street number for their address. For example: **29 W. Bottlecap Alley, Antsodea** (29 is the student's number). I also use this number for many classroom management purposes.

Draw a simple map of the classroom on the overhead or chalkboard. As a class brainstorm names for the major paths of traffic in the room. You can have streets, avenues, alleys, boulevards, or highways, depending on your room set-up.

I let the students name the streets they live on. Don't forget to name your street.

Hire one of the students to make a nice black-line master of the map. Pay the student with the society's currency. Duplicate the map for parents and guests so they don't get lost in your room! As the society progresses, students like to make maps that show where each business is located. Ask a creative parent to make street signs that can stand or hang in the classroom.

Check out Antsodea's map on the next page. Use the change of address form on page 22 if a student moves.

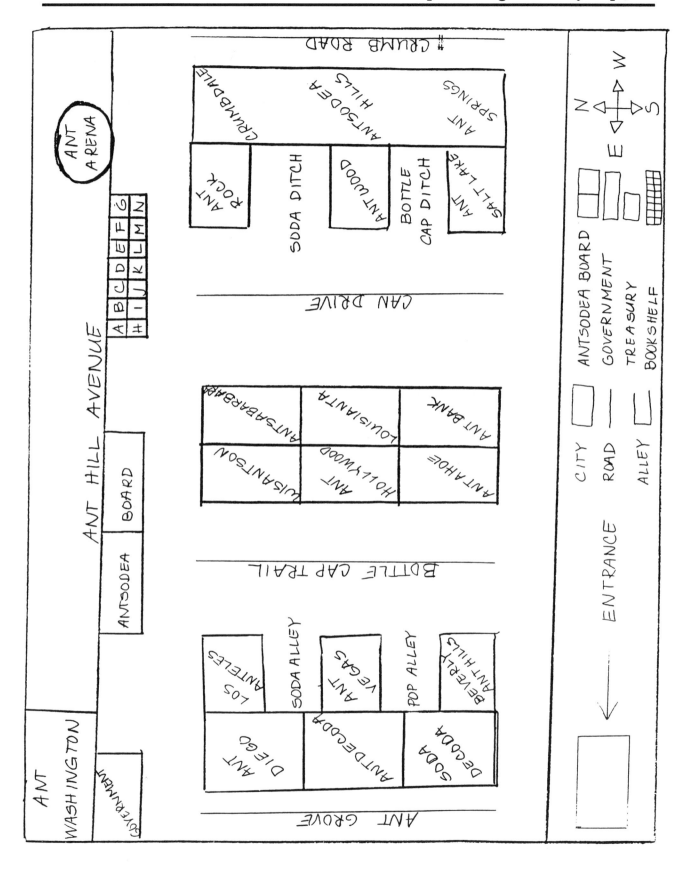

Change of Address Form

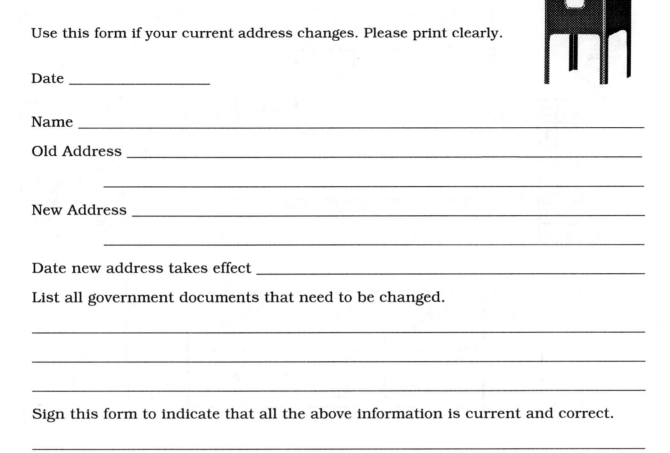

Use this form if your current address changes. Please print clearly.

Date _____

Name _____

Old Address _____

_____

New Address _____

_____

Date new address takes effect _____

List all government documents that need to be changed.

_____

_____

_____

Sign this form to indicate that all the above information is current and correct.

_____

Step 12
Odds and Ends

As the society progresses, you will discover lots of fun artifacts unique to the society. Here are some samples and ideas:

1. An official stamp to stamp all official documents, like licenses

2. Visa stamps for passports

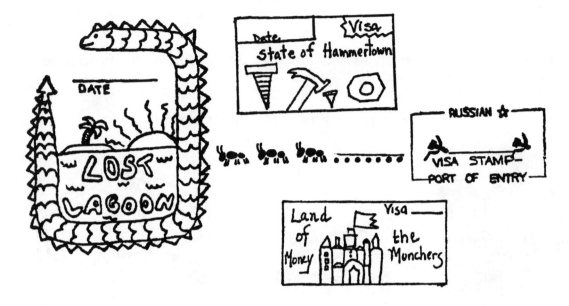

3. An official bird or flower

4. Hall passes—for Tropical Island, we had starfish and blow-up palm trees

5. Letterhead for documents

6. Banners and door signs

7. Various artifacts that represent the society, such as visors, hats, magnets, plaster statues, necklaces, clothing, decorations, or pencils

You will find a great sense of pride develop as unique society artifacts are adopted. We had lots of fun with the Tropical Island theme; the kids found shirts, tennis shoes, earrings, and all sorts of things that could easily represent Tropical Island.

Phase II
Setting Up the Society

You have developed the basic spirit and environment of your society. Now it's time to build the foundation for the social studies, economics, and other integrated disciplines that the society will encompass after it is fully functioning. This foundation also organizes classroom management, which will direct the society and classroom.

In this phase, classroom and government jobs will be researched, a pay scale will be developed, job applications will be filled out, employees will be hired and trained, ledgers will be started, checking accounts may be opened, citizen identification cards will be made, and students will experience their first payday within the society.

Step 1
Classroom and School Jobs

Classroom jobs are jobs you need students to do to make the classroom run smoothly. School jobs are jobs students can do to help the school function. School jobs include cafeteria workers, student council representatives, and others.

As a class, brainstorm a list of classroom jobs and school jobs. Or if you already have a list of jobs you'd like to delegate, pass out the list.

Here is a sample list of jobs:

2 Art Monitors

1 Attendance Monitor

1 Ball Monitor

2 Cafeteria Workers

2 Custodians

2 Classroom Librarians

1 Door/Light Monitor

1 Flag Monitor

2 Homework Check-ins

2 Line Leaders

1 Lunch Ticket Taker

2 Mail Carriers

3 Make-up Monitors

1 Media Technician

1 Miscellaneous Monitor

2 Office Messengers

2 Overhead Monitors

2 Paper Monitors

2 School Librarians

1 Secretary

2 Substitutes

2 Student Council Representatives

1 Telephone Operator

2 Telecommunicators

Some students will work alone, others will work in pairs.

Because I need students to start doing classroom jobs right away, I ask for volunteers and write their names on the list next to the jobs they will be doing.

If you prefer to have students apply for the jobs before you hire them, use the job application form on page 28. After you have assigned the jobs, have the students research their new jobs by getting information from you or other students who have had similar jobs in the past.

Have students fill in a job description worksheet on page 29. Collect the completed job descriptions in a booklet for student reference. (Or you may write the job descriptions and hand them out.)

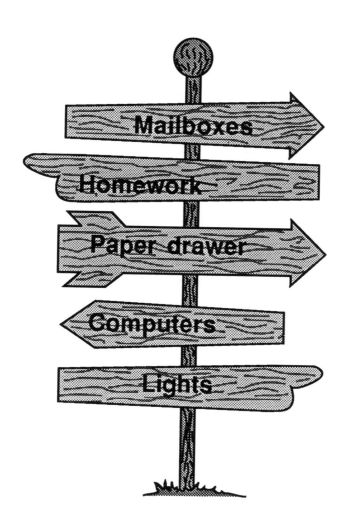

Classroom/School Job Application

Name _____ Date _____

List 3 jobs you would like to have.

1st choice _____

2nd choice _____

3rd choice _____

Why do you think you are qualified or want each job?

1st choice _____

2nd choice _____

3rd choice _____

Do you have any previous experience with your . . .

1st choice _____

2nd choice _____

3rd choice _____

Your signature indicates that all the above information is correct.

_____

Job Description

Name _____ Date _____

Name of job _____

How much time this job takes daily _____ x 5 = weekly _____

Briefly describe the job. _____

_____

_____

_____

List the major responsibilities.

1. _____

2. _____

3. _____

4. _____

5. _____

6. _____

7. _____

Step 2
Government Jobs

Government jobs facilitate the overall management of the society. To start, you will need these basic government jobs:

2 Treasurers—Keep the books for all the government monies and distribute weekly salaries to the Pay Processors

5-6 Pay Processors—Keep track of their assigned students' weekly pay and pay them

2-3 Money Cutters—Cut the society's money for the treasury

2 Auction Officials—Coordinate the auction and keep it running smoothly

3-4 Auction Secretaries—Record the sales information for the auctions

If and when you feel your students are ready, you can introduce checks and checkbooks. At this point, you will need to add these government jobs:

1 Bank President—Runs each citizen's bank statement every two weeks. Delivers the statements to each Pay Processor. Assists the Operations Manager and Bank Tellers as needed.

1 Operations Manager—Checks the Bank Tellers' accuracy and the Pay Processors' records. Assists the Bank President as necessary.

5 Bank Tellers—Each bank teller is assigned one day of the week. They enter all the bank transactions for the students assigned to their day.

1 ATM Teller—Available to cash paychecks and personal checks throughout the week.

2 Payroll Clerks—Replace the treasurer in the basic government jobs. Responsible for writing the paychecks and distributing them to the Pay Processors on their specific payday.

See appendix B for complete job descriptions that can be copied and handed out to the students. Let students study the job descriptions before they apply for a job.

Step 3
The Pay Scale

It is necessary to make an official pay scale for the society using the list of jobs and their descriptions. Most of my societies voted on pay according to the time it takes to do a particular job. They usually add a little more pay to the jobs with the most responsibility. Create your pay scale before you actually hire students for the positions.

In drafting a pay scale, you need to warn students about inflation. If students start with large amounts of money (i.e., $1,000 per week for salaries), money management will be cumbersome and prices of products will be unusually high. Encourage students to keep salaries, taxes, and payments low. Calculate possible weekly salaries to keep things in perspective. The sample pay scales are a feasible starting place.

As a class have students brainstorm everything they want to get paid for and charged for, such as doing or not doing their homework. From this unfolds a positive and effective classroom management and discipline plan.

As a facilitator, record the ideas, allow for discussion, and keep things moving.

After the society adopts a pay scale, type and duplicate it so that every citizen has a copy for reference. I put one copy in each student's individual file, along with the student's ledger (see step 7).

Page 32 shows a pay scale adopted in a classroom that used checkbooks, and page 33 shows an example adopted in a classroom that did not use checkbooks. These examples may help you generate ideas, but remember, foster your own uniqueness. Kids are very creative when challenged!

Lost Lagoon Pay Scale

Adopted 9/24/1993

JOBS

A **(15 min./week)**	**B** **(30 min./week)**	**C** **(45 min./week)**	**D** **(60 min./week)**
Flag Monitor	Paper Monitor	ATM Teller	Bank President
Ball Monitor	Secretary	Auction Official	Bank Teller
Telecommunicator	Homework Check-in	Art Monitor	Operations Manager
Substitute	Auction Secretary		Pay Processor
School and	Media Technician		Cafeteria Worker
Classroom Librarians			
Attendance Monitor	Custodian		
Miscellaneous Monitor	Payroll Clerk		
Overhead Monitor	Mail Carrier		
Telephone Operator	Door/Light Monitor		

Make-up Monitor and Money Cutter salaries vary
Admiral, Skipper & Mates +7 per day

Job Pay Scale

A	**B**	**C**	**D**
10 SD/week	15 SD/week	20 SD/week	25 SD/week
2 SD/day	3 SD/day	4 SD/day	5 SD/day

SD=Sandollars

Income

Charger/4 weeks	10 SD
Completed Homework	3 SD/day
Good Behavior	2 SD/day (no name in book)
Weekly challenge	2 SD
Accurate checkbook	3 SD
Clean desk	3 SD

SD=Sandollars

Taxes

No name on paper	-5 SD	Demerits	-5 SD
No number on paper	-5 SD	Bathroom	-5 SD
Name in book (behavior)	-3 SD	Drink	-3 SD
Each check	-5 SD	Pencil sharpened	-1 SD
Blue slip	-10 SD	Out of line	-5 SD
No homework	-6 SD	Messy desk	-5 SD
Bail	(teacher sets)		
Bounced check	-7 SD		

SD=Sandollars

Castle Rock Pay Scale
Adopted 9/21/1992
JOBS

A
(<15 min./day)
Cafeteria Workers
Catcher-upper
Paper Monitors
Treasurer
Pay Processors
Auction Official
Auction Secretary
Student Council Representatives

B
(10-15 min./day)
Art Monitors
School Librarian
Homework Checking
Mail Carriers
Maintenance
Miscellaneous Monitor
Overhead Monitors
Paper Monitors

C
(1-9 min./day)
Ball Monitors
Classroom Librarian
Door/Light Monitor
Flag Monitor
Lunch Ticket Taker
Telecommunicators
Telephone Operator
Word-of-Week Monitor

Substitutes make the same salary as those for whom they sub.

Job Pay Scale

A
15 RR/week
3 each day

B
10 RR/week
2 each day

C
5 RR/week
1 each day

RR=Royal Rubies

Income

Charger/4 weeks	5 RR
Completed Homework	3 RR/day
Good Behavior	3 RR/day (no name in book)
Good Attendance	10 RR/monthly
No PE Demerit	3 RR/2 weeks
No blue slips	3 RR/2 weeks
Clean desk	3 RR/weekly

RR=Royal Rubies

Taxes

No name on paper	-5	Demerits	-5
No number on paper	-2	Bathroom	-5
Name in book (behavior)	-3	Drink	-2
Each check	-5	Pencil sharpened	-1
Blue slip	-5	Out of line	-5
No homework	-6	Messy desk	-1
Bail	(teacher sets)		

RR=Royal Rubies

Step 4
Seeking Employment

It's time for employment lines! Provide each student seeking a government job with a General Job Application from appendix C. I allow students a couple of days to research the jobs (use the job descriptions from appendix B) and fill out the general application. Encourage students to attach letters of recommendation and copies of report cards to their applications. Remind them to apply for more than one job in case they don't get their first choice.

There are two ways you can handle job applications:

1. Copy the job application form from appendix C and distribute them. Allow a set amount of time to complete the applications.

2. Hold a job fair. Set up booths and have students wait in line to fill out applications. Set up at least three booths per type of job application. Hang up signs and have fun with it.

Let students know that job notification will be within 48 hours after you collect the completed job applications.

Step 5
Employees Hired

After you read through all the applications, select the best candidate(s) for each job. I use a yellow marker to highlight each student's "selling" points so each student can see why he or she got the job. You can use another color to mark areas that cost a student a job. Students can learn a great deal from this. Make it as positive as possible. With the many classroom and government jobs available, everyone in your room should have a job. This is important for building self-esteem.

Depending on how much time you want to spend, you can either (1) interview students and tell them why they were hired, or (2) post a hiring list. I have used both methods, and both are effective.

Staple the job description from appendix B to a copy of the form on page 36. Pass them out to your new staff!

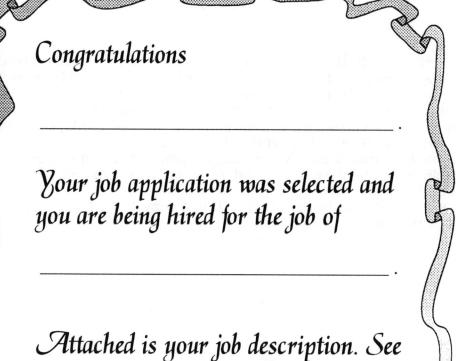

Congratulations

_____ .

Your job application was selected and you are being hired for the job of

_____ .

Attached is your job description. See you at our training meeting.

I know you'll do a fine job!!

From *The Mini-Society Workbook.* © 1996. Teacher Ideas Press. (800) 237-6124.

Step 6
Train Your Government Employees

Your government employees will benefit from some individual training. Make them feel professional by planning a special meeting just for them—lunchtime in your room, after school, or during an independent activity. You won't need to train your auction employees until two weeks before the first auction. I find it easier to train them in the following groups:

1. Money Cutters and Payroll Clerks or Treasurers

2. Bank President, Operations Manager, and Tellers

3. Pay Processors and substitute Pay Processors along with Bank President and Operations Manager

4. Auction Officials and Auction Secretaries

Some Training Tips

ATM Teller

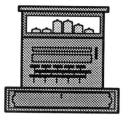

Materials needed:

job description (appendix B)

file box with a lock and key (cash box)

lined composition book (to record transactions)

Cash Only stamp and stamp pad

Special instructions:

Help the ATM Teller set up the transactions book as shown:

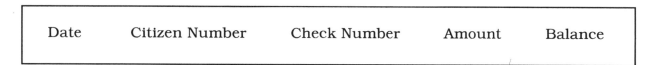

Date	Citizen Number	Check Number	Amount	Balance

Train the ATM Teller to look for proper endorsement of the checks and to stamp *Cash Only* on the front of each check. When the ATM Teller needs more cash, the teacher will provide it and the teller will enter it as a deposit. The teller needs to try to keep the books balanced.

Auction Officials

Quiet on the Auction floor!

Materials needed:

job description (appendix B)

lined composition book (to record auctions)

container with each citizen's number on it

permission to auction sheets (appendix D)

Special instructions:

Help Auction Officials set up their composition book as shown:

Name of Auction Official (they can rotate responsibility)
Date of Auction

Number of Seller	Item	Starting Bid	Auctioneer Number	Secretary Number

---

They will make an individual sheet for each auction. Rotate the Auction Secretary to every third or fourth seller. Familiarize Auction Officials with the rules of an auction (see phase IV, step 1). It is important that they collect permission slips for each seller; sellers without permission slips can't auction.

Auction Secretaries

Materials needed:

job description (appendix B)

lined composition book (to record sales)

Special instructions:

The name of the secretary should be written on the outside of the book. Help Auction Secretaries set up their composition books as shown:

Date of Auction	Seller Number	Buyer Number	Selling Price	Paid

---

The auctioneer will hand the item to the Auction Secretary, who will collect the money from the buyer, hand the item to the buyer, and pay the seller.

Bank President

Materials needed:

job description (appendix B)

file box (use a legal-sized check filing box from a stationary store)

an accounting computer program such as Checkbook by Interact.

Special instructions:

You may want the Bank President to attend all the other training meetings to learn all the processes involved. You will need to provide hands-on software training for the Bank President and the Operations Manager. Take them through the computer program step by step, teaching them how to run bank statements. After they run the bank statements and staple the paperwork to them, have them clear the account in the computer, leaving only the ending balances for each citizen.

Bank Tellers

Materials needed:

job description (appendix B)

6 boxes (5 "In" boxes (one for each teller) and 1 "Out" box for all tellers to share)

Entered stamp, date stamp, and stamp pad

a checkbook computer program such as Checkbook from Interact

Special instructions:

The bank tellers will need hands-on training so they can enter deposits and withdrawals for each account accurately. Assign each teller one day of the week. Each teller will have an In box and an assigned list of citizens who will put their transactions in their teller's In box. Tellers will need to write their initials and stamp each transaction with the Entered stamp and the date stamp. Their completed work is placed in the Out box. Stress accuracy!!

Money Cutters

Materials needed:

job description (appendix B)

file folder with student's name on it

copies of the Money Cutter Contract (appendix D)

medium-sized manila envelope to store cut money in

10 sheets of the society's printed money

Special instructions:

Hand out the students' individual folders with the first allotment of money to cut. Explain the contract and their responsibilities. Any money they lose will come out of their own salary. Have them fill out and sign their first contract.

Operations Manager

Materials needed:

job description (appendix B)

calculator

sample Pay Processor Sheet (appendix D)

overhead transparency of the Pay Processor Sheet (appendix D)

Special instructions:

You may want to have the Operations Manager attend the Pay Processors' training meeting, because the Operations Manager will be checking the Pay Processors' work. Use the overhead transparency to illustrate what a Pay Processor might record for a week. Teach the Operations Manager to use a calculator to check the Pay Processors' work. Go through examples. They will need to make any corrections with a red pen and initial the sheet.

Pay Processors

Materials needed:

job description (appendix B)

1 file folder for each Pay Processor (list the names of citizens assigned to that Pay Processor on the front of the folder. Staple the pay scale on the left inside flap.)

Pay Processor Sheets for each citizen (appendix D)

overhead transparency of Pay Processor Sheet (appendix D)

calculator

Special instructions:

Assign each Pay Processor an even number of students and a day of the week that will be their payday. Don't forget yourself and any other adults who regularly work in the classroom! I have found it helpful to assign to Pay Processors students who sit close to them.

Explain how to fill out the Pay Processor Sheets properly. The Pay Processors will complete the Pay Processor Sheets each day. Use the overhead transparency to create examples to solve. For example, Peter did his homework on Monday, Tuesday, and Wednesday, but not on Thursday. He got a check on Tuesday and a drink on Wednesday. He went to the bathroom on Thursday. He did his job, which was worth $10. Using the pay scale, figure out what his week's salary was.

Emphasize accuracy and responsibility. If the Pay Processors are frequently absent, they won't be able to keep their job. When they are absent, a substitute Pay Processor should always be able to find their folder and will earn their pay for that day.

Sample Pay Processor Sheet:

Pay Processor _Jessica Bibeau_ of _Deanna Barkley_

Address _#2 Surfers Alley_

Jobs _Homework check-in_   Salary _6_

Pay Processor   _8_

Subject	Mon.	Tues.	Wed.	Thurs.	Fri.
homework	X	+3	+3	+3	+3
behavior	+3	+3	+1	+3	+3
job				+6	
job				+8	
taxes					
taxes					
other					
other					
Daily Totals	+3	+6		+20	+6

Date paid _FEB 04 PAID_   Grand Total _+39_   Treasurer's Initials _RV_

Payroll Clerks

Materials needed:

job description (appendix B)

lined composition book (ledger for check information)

paycheck box (file box to store blank paychecks)

blank copies of society's paychecks (appendix D)

calculator

Special instructions:
Help the Payroll Clerks set up their books as shown:

Date	Citizen Number	Check Number	Amount

The Payroll Clerks may design the society's checks or use the form in appendix D. They need to number the checks consecutively and always make sure there are plenty of checks.

They *do not* have to keep a running total after writing each check. Instead, they put the written checks in the Pay Processors' folders and return them to the Pay Processor each day.

Treasurers

Materials needed:

job description (appendix B)

lined composition book (Treasury Book)

date stamp (the kind you find in stationary stores)

stamp pad (can use society's colors)

file box with a lock and key (for the money)

calculator

Special instructions:
Help your treasurers set up the Treasury Book as shown:

Date	Deposit	Withdrawal	Reason	Balance

Teach notation for the basic entries:

When money is deposited, enter it in the deposit column with a + sign in front of it.

When money is withdrawn, enter it in the withdrawal column with a - sign in front of it.

Illustrate various reasons for deposits and withdrawals:

1. Deposits
   a. Treasury deposit (record initials of Money Cutters making the deposit)
   b. Tax deposit (record tax being paid, such as messy desk, and the name of the person paying the tax)

2. Withdrawals
   a. To Pay Processors (enter the abbreviation PP and the initials of the Pay Processor receiving the money)
   b. For public relations or government expenses (state the reason and to whom the money is given)

Sample of a treasury book from Tropical Island:

Date	Deposit	Withdrawal	Reason	Bal.
¹¹/₆	4,650		Treasury Deposit	4,650
NOV 12 ENT'D	4,650		Treasury Deposit	4,650
NOV 16 ENT'D				9,300
	4,630		Treasury Deposit	4,630
				13,930
NOV 16 ENT'D		-115	Jeff - P.M.	- 115
				13,815
NOV 16 ENT'D		- 73	Deanna - P.M.	- 73
				13,742

Step 7
Personal Ledgers

Before the first payday can take place, students need to learn how to keep a personal ledger. This is a ledger that allows them to keep track of all their money. In case of a loss, I make them show me their ledger to verify how much money they had. (If you use checkbooks, skip to step 7a.)

Pass out a file folder to each student. On the outside they'll write their name and address. Staple the pay scale on the left flap and a Personal Ledger Sheet (appendix D) on the right inside flap. Make an overhead transparency of the personal ledger form to use in instructing the whole class.

Teach the types of entries they will most likely use:

Types of Entries	Notation	Types of Transactions
Payday	+	deposit
Business earnings	+	deposit
Tax or fine	−	withdrawal
Purchase	−	withdrawal

The ledgers should allow room to add and subtract and to enter balances. Students need to use their calculators and record every transaction to keep their accounts accurate. Check their filled ledger sheet briefly each time they are ready for another ledger sheet. Initial their sheet and staple the new ledger sheet on top of the old one.

Example of a ledger and it's entries:

Raymond's Personal Ledger

Date	Description received from or paid to	Deposit (+)	Withdrawal (−)	Balance
				1,291
4/11/88	from Mrs. F. drawing	+50		+ 50
				1,341
4/15/88	from Jeff payday	+33		+ 33
				1,374
4/15/88	paid business day		− 35	− 35
				1,339
4/16/88	paid to Michael auction		− 305	− 305
				1,034
4/22/88	from Jeff payday	+42		+ 42
				1,076

Step 7a
Checkbook Registers

If you use checkbooks, have students bring in a blank checkbook register to use. With the checkbook method, students don't have to keep track of their cash, just the money they deposit into their checking account to write checks or withdraw as cash. This makes recordkeeping a lot easier. Classroom calculators are a real asset here!

Make an overhead transparency of a checkbook register page to use in instructing the whole class.

Teach the types of entries they will most likely use:

Types of Checks	Notation	Types of Transactions
Paycheck	+	deposit
Checks from others	+	deposit
Checks they write	−	withdrawal
Checks for cash	−	withdrawal

Students need to be reminded to skip every other line to allow room to calculate their balances. They do not do this naturally. Remind them to use their calculators for accuracy.

Example of a checkbook register:

*USE THESE CODES WHEN RECORDING YOUR NON-CHECK TRANSACTIONS D-DEPOSIT DC-DEBIT CARD ATM-TELLER MACHINE AP-AUTOMATIC PAYMENT TT-TELEPHONE TRANSFER O-OTHER									
CHECK NUMBER	DATE	* TRAN'S TYPE	DESCRIPTION OF TRANSACTION	PAYMENT/DEBIT (—)	FEE (—)	✓ TAX	DEPOSIT/CREDIT (+)	BALANCE FWD. $365	00
	2/2		Deposit Payday	$			$ +40 00	+40 405	00 00
32	2/4		L.L. gov Bathroom tax	− 5 00				−5 400	00 00
	2/9		Deposit Payday				+ 35 00	+35 435	00 00
33	2/10		Cash for business day	− 55 00				−55 380	00 00
34	2/14		admiral Fletcher no name + # on paper	− 10 00				− 10 370	00 00
	2/16		Deposit Payday				+ 40 00	+40 410	00 00

Deposit and check writing will need to be taught. Use overhead transparencies of a deposit slip and a check (appendix D), to illustrate the concepts. Once again, stress accuracy!

Sample deposit slip:

ADMIRAL FLETCHER
28 NORTH ADMIRABLE QUARTERS
SANDBARS
LOST LAGOON 37374

DEPOSIT RECORD

_1-13_ 19 _94_

CHECKS	AMOUNT
#7-	$15.00
paycheck #343	$45.00
	$60.00

Tell students to attach the money they are depositing to the deposit slip with a paper clip and place the deposit in their designated payday box. The Bank Teller then enters the deposit into the computer.

Teach basic check-writing skills. You may need to have a special spelling lesson to practice money amounts, for example, twenty-one dollars.

Students will need to make sure they number all their checks and record each accurately in their checkbook registers. What a great skill to learn. Adults have trouble with this! I have had students manage a checkbook better than their parents!

Sample check:

ADMIRAL FLETCHER
28 NORTH ADMIRABLE QUARTERS
SANDBARS
LOST LAGOON   37374

CHECK NUMBER 12

_1-12_ 19 _94_

PAY TO THE
ORDER OF _Nicole Houston_ $ _30.00_

Thirty sandollars and no/100- DOLLARS

LOST LAGOON BANK AND TRUST

FOR _auction item_

Admiral Fletcher
ADMIRAL FLETCHER

ACCT. #28   ENTERED ___

Every two weeks bank statements will be handed out to reconcile. It is easiest to teach this skill when students receive their first bank statement. Make it a whole class project. Sample bank statement:

LOST LAGOON BANK AND TRUST
CHECKING ACCOUNT STATEMENT FOR:

ACCOUNT #: 28

ADMIRAL FLETCHER
28 NORTH ADMIRABLE QUARTERS
SANDBARS, LOST LOGOON 37374

DATE: 5/15/94

BALANCE FORWARD $22270

NUMBER	BALANCE		CHECK	DEPOSIT
26	2120		150	
27	2110		10	
28	2085		25	
29	2055		30	
DEPOSIT		2100		45
30	2085		15	
DEPOSIT		2125		40
SVC CHG			5.00	

ENDING BALANCE = 2120

I found the following stamp to help students reconcile their bank statements. I use in on the back of their statements to make the process easier. You can have a stamp made or purchase one from an office supply store.

BANK RECONCILIATION

Bank Statement Balance _____	Check Book Balance _____
Deposits Not Credited _____	
+_____	Service Charge -_____
Total _____	Adjusted Check Book Balance _____
Total Outstanding Checks -_____	
Adjusted Bank Balance _____	

You may also use the special bank statement reconciliation form in appendix D.
Lead students through the process of reconciling their bank statements step by step. Remind them of the $5 service charge and $5 charge for each bounced check!

If students find an error, they need to fill out a Checkbook Adjustment Form (appendix D).

After students balance their statements, I have them draw a line in their checkbook registers and record the date balanced. I check them and initial their register.

Step 8
Preparation for the First Payday

To get ready for the first payday, you will need to do the following:

1. Get samples of colored paper that can be used for the society's money. They should match colors chosen in Phase I. You can get neat neon colors from stationary stores. Students will vote on the color of their choice.

2. If the office staff is going to copy the money for you, be sure to ask them to enclose a bill so you can pay them when you pick up the completed job. (This will whet their appetite to get in on the action!)

Bill of sale for copying of currency:

```
┌──────────────────────────────────────────────────┐
│              United   Nations                      │
│ Feb.  23,  1988                                    │
│       Materials........................... 5 shells│
│       Labor.............................15 shells  │
│                              20  shells            │
│ Due  and  payable  upon  receipt  of  completed job.│
│       United Nations office staff                  │
└──────────────────────────────────────────────────┘
```

3. Copy the money. I have found that the best way to do this is to group four drawings each of ones, fives, tens, twenties, fifties, and hundreds on separate sheets. Then run off the following numbers of copies:

Denomination	Number of Sheets (four bills per sheet)
Ones	100
Fives	80
Tens	80
Twenties	80
Fifties	60
Hundreds	100

4. If you are using checks as well as currency, run off one-half the suggested amount of currency and make sure the payroll clerk is ready with an ample supply of paychecks (1 per citizen per week).

5. After the money is cut, have it deposited in treasury.

49

Step 9
The First Payday

Are you ready for fewer discipline problems?

Assign each Pay Processor one day of the week. Pay Processors need to have their Pay Processor Sheets for each of their assigned citizens ready to go on their designated day. Usually, your top students are the Pay Processors, and you'll find paydays don't interfere with other curricula at all. My students usually do it after they're done with their reading.

Here's the plan of attack for payday:

1. The Treasurers or Payroll Clerks set up an area with the treasury, Treasury Book (ledger), calculator, and date stamp.

2. The Pay Processor for that day gives his or her folder to the Treasurers or Payroll Clerks.

3. The Treasurers or Payroll Clerks put each citizen's earned income with their Pay Processor Sheet and give the folder back to the Pay Processor.

4. The Pay Processors quietly pay their assigned citizens.

5. If a citizen is absent, the Pay Processor is responsible for the money until the citizen returns to school.

6. If a citizen owes the treasury money, he or she pays the Pay Processor, who gives the money to the Treasurer or ATM Teller.

If debts occur in the very beginning of the society, have students either pay it in minutes after school or work it off in some way. Don't let a student go too far into debt!

If a student is in debt, he or she can't buy goods or privileges until the debt is paid off. Believe me, as money attains its value in the society, students will be highly motivated to be on their best behavior! It can be expensive otherwise!!

Step 10
Citizenship Cards

On a 5-x-8-inch Citizenship Card, have the students fill out information about themselves. Keep the cards in a file box labeled Citizenship Cards. It is important for students to keep their cards current.

Example of a Citizenship Card:

> *Name*
> *Address (society address)*
> *Current jobs and salaries*
> *Names of businesses*

If you want to do W-2s and income tax returns in April, have students add the following information to their cards in January:

> *Amount of personal income made from September to January*
> *List of current businesses and total profit from September to January*
> *Current balance in ledger (if using checkbooks, include cash on hand)*

These cards are government files and may be used in the society's court system or by private investigators! They also may help Pay Processors if jobs or addresses change.

Phase III
Getting Down to Business

Enthusiasm is mounting, and the society is ready to progress further by opening classroom businesses. Once in a while there may be a student who isn't interested in attaining wealth in the society and doesn't really care if he or she has to pay for not doing homework. As businesses flourish, the money attains much more value, and you will see this attitude disappear!

Be a role model in this phase by getting involved in the action and setting up your own business. I have found it really fun to get the office staff and parents involved. It generates even more value to the system.

Have fun shopping!

Step 1
A Business Idea

Sometimes, it is hard for students to come up with business ideas. Channel their thinking toward things they can make or small items they can buy with earned money. Be sensitive to the student that has a hard time coming up with an idea. I usually wait a couple of business days before I start to give suggestions to the student who still hasn't gotten off the ground.

I have found it helpful to talk about former societies' businesses with the students. When I first did this, I was afraid the past societies' businesses would be duplicated. A few were, but I always have new, unique businesses every year. As in the real world, the market changes constantly, and different things are popular from year to year.

For some reason, students think that if one student opens a "friendship bracelet" business, another student can't. "Why not?" I say. "That's how it is in the real world!"

You may need to emphasize that everything sold must be legal and within the school rules. For example, if Pogs™ are not allowed on school grounds, then a Pog store can't be opened.

Newspapers are a real asset. My first societies used the software Newsroom to create their society newspapers; later societies used the Children's Writing Center. My mother wrote an advice column for a sixth-grade newspaper. The kids loved it and got to meet the mystery columnist at the culmination ceremony.

The following lists summarize businesses started in three of my Mini-Societies. Following these lists, additional ideas for businesses are offered.

Cryton's Businesses

Alice's Fruit Stand
Angela's Bank
Carla's Treasure Shop (junk)
Checkers
Cryton Branch Library
Cryton's Hiring Service
Eva's Typewriter Service
Helen's Investment Co. (loans)
Major School Supplies
Miglet's Snack Bar (Popcorn & Pickles)
Pab's Drinks

Pablo's Pizzeria
Pencil Can
Puzzle & Crosswords
Record Rental
Rent an Auctioneer
The Rosery House (roses)
Stickers
Trinh's School Supply Shop
Weekly Central (newspaper)
Zebra (a logic game)

Antsodea's Businesses

AntSo. Bank
Antsodea Times (newspaper)
Can Drive Snack Shop (chips,
    granola bars, fun fruits)
Delicious Pickles
Eduardo's Corn Nut Shop
Elaine's Eraser Shop
Hot Sticks (Health Department
    of Antsodea closed this one)
Jeff's Cooler (punch)
Lottery Tickets
Magical Book Shop
Monika's Cards

Muffin House (blueberry)
Nicole's Checks
Peanut Butter Boppers
Popcorn Palace
Rent-a-Pencil
Ruben's Pencil Shop
Sal's Salted Lemons
Salted Plums
Souvenirs (flags, banners,
    pillows, and beanbags)
Stationary
Stickers & Art Shop

Tropical Island's Businesses

Braceletland (bracelets)
C&M Skater Shop (pictures, bracelets, stickers)
Cookieland
Crazy Containers (boxes, bags, and the like)
Fine Yarn & Pictures
Geography Lottery (parent business)
Golden State International Bank
Island Punch
Junk & Used Toy Shop
Little Lighthouse (clay)
Mike's Wallets
Music for Your Ears (like a juke box, pay per song)
Pencil Shop
Pictureland (drawings)
Tandy Taffy
Teddy Bear Shop (stuffed animals)
Totally Tubular Souvenirs
Tropical Alley's Lawyer's office
Tropical Bookmarks
Tropical Cards
Tropical Cowhides (an art project)
Tropical Island National Bank
Tropical Savings
Tropical Stickers
Tropical Times (newspaper)
Yummy to Your Tummy Bakery

More Business Ideas

address books
barrettes
baseball cards
bookmarks
bubble bath
buttons (use a button machine)
catch n' play (water bottles cut in
    half and tennis balls)
cheese and crackers
computer games
computer-generated stationary,
    banners, and so on
decorated clothespin magnets
decorated pencils
door hangers
dried flower arrangements
dried fruit
earrings
face painting
fish tanks (use liter bottles)
fresh flowers
halos
jacks and balls
Jacob's ladders (a wooden flip-flap toy)
little baskets

mazes
origami
painted combs
painted wooden figures
personalized cups and containers
photo booth (backdrops to
    have photos taken)
pinwheels
plants
Playdoh
rock people (painted rocks with
    decorations or sayings glued on)
safety pins decorated with beads
sand paintings in jars
seasonal crafts
Silly Putty
society newspaper
spices (in netting)
spin art
stress busters (balloons filled with
    flour or salt)
temporary tattoos
tic-tac-toe games
wooden necklaces

Step 2
The Market Survey

After the students have been given a chance to formulate their business ideas, conduct a Market Survey, which will allow them to get their Business License and open a business. Forms for use in this activity appear on the following five pages.

In the market survey, students are responsible for:

1. **Assessing the demand.** Students fill out Form A to find out whether their product is appealing to their peers. I encourage students to make a sample of their product to show students. They can pass their sample and Form A around in class while working on other assignments, or you can allow a time for everyone to assess the demand at the same time.

2. **Graphing the results.** If the majority of the responses were positive, then students can fill out Form B (page 59), based on data recorded on Form A.

3. **Proposing the business.** This involves planning exactly what the business is. Students complete Form C (page 60).

4. **Discussing the business with their parents.** Students discuss with their parents their proposed business and how they intend to finance it. Parents approve the idea and financing by signing Form D (page 61).

5. **Applying for the business license.** This is the final task! Students fill out Form E (page 62) and staple it to the front of Forms A-D. They turn in all forms to an area that you have designated for that purpose.

Post a sign that says:

PLEASE ALLOW 48 HOURS FOR THE PROCESSING OF YOUR APPLICATIONS.

Assessing the Demand
(Form A)

Name _____ Date _____

I am going to sell _____

Briefly describe it _____

Will you buy it? Put a number under Yes or No and circle it.

Yes	No

How much would you be willing to pay for it?
(Put a tally mark under the one you choose.)

1-5	6-10	11-20	21-50	51-100

Graphing the Results
(Form B)

Name _____ Date _____

Use the data you gathered on Form A to complete these graphs.

Number of Responses

50
45
40
35
30
25
20
15
10
5

Yes   No

Type of Response

Number of Responses

50
45
40
35
30
25
20
15
10
5

(1-5) (6-10) (11-20) (21-50) (51-100)

Amount Willing to Pay

Proposing the Business
(Form C)

Name _____ Date _____

Address _____

_____

Name of proposed business _____

Product(s) you will sell _____

_____

Approximate price(s) of your products _____

List the materials you will need to make your product(s). Circle those you will have to buy with real money.

_____ _____ _____ _____

_____ _____ _____ _____

_____ _____ _____ _____

_____ _____ _____ _____

_____ _____ _____ _____

Explain how you're going to finance your business.

_____

_____

_____

Parent Contract
(Form D)

Circle your choice: a, b, or c.

I, _____ , of _____ business

(a) have agreed to _____ for my parent(s) in exchange for

$_____ , which I will use to finance my business.

or

(b) am going to use my allowance to finance my business.

or

(c) will need _____

_____

from home to make my business product.

To the student: Explain to your parent(s) your business idea.
To the parent: If this is okay with you, please sign and have your child return it to school for his/her Business License.

___ ___ ___ ___ ___ ___ ___ ___ ___ ___ ___ ___ ___ ___ ___ ___ ___ ___

_____   _____
(Student's signature)   (Parent's signature)

Application for the Business License
(Form E)

PLEASE PRINT CLEARLY

Name _____ Date _____

Legal name of your business _____

Business address _____

_____

Type of product(s) you're selling _____

_____

(Instruction: Staple Forms A-D to the back of this form. Allow 48 hours for the processing of your application. Thank you.)

Step 3
Issuing the Business License and Lease

Review each application. If there are components missing or things you feel won't work, send it back with corrections. I write my comments on the bottom of Form E (for example, "Form A is incomplete").

For the applications that are satisfactory, speak to the students individually to congratulate them and and issue their license and lease agreement. I usually provide the first license free as an incentive to get a business started.

Students need to read all business documents carefully before signing them. Stress that the license must be displayed when they are conducting business and that they cannot sell outside business hours or without a license.

The land they lease is their desk, unless they need to lease special furniture in the classroom. (That costs extra!)

If they lose their license, they will have to pay a fee and fill out another Form E.

I like to glue the license onto a piece of construction paper (use the society's color) and stamp it with the official society stamp. After the licenses are signed, laminate them. Staple the lease to the student's other business documents (Forms A-E) and file them.

Business License

Name of merchant/s __Empress Fletcher__

Name of Business __Fletcher's Funny Farm__

Business Address __33 S. Empress Lane__

__Crystal Canyon, Cedargrove L2945__

Product/s sold __logic games__

I hereby promise to engage in legal business operations at all times and abide by the business regulations established by __Crystal Canyon__

__Empress Fletcher__
(Owner's signature)

__Empress Fletcher__
(teacher's signature)

Crystal Canyon

Display During Business Hours

Business License
Display During Business Hours

Name of merchant(s) _____

Name of business _____

Business address _____

_____

Product(s) sold _____

I hereby promise to engage in legal business operations at all times and abide by the business regulations established by

_____ .

_____
(Owner's signature)

_____
(Teacher's signature)

Lease Agreement

I _____ of _____ business
   (name of merchant)   (name of business)

accept the lease for the land located at _____
                                              (business address)

for the sale of my merchandise. I agree to pay _____
                                                    (amount)

on the first Friday of each month to the treasury of _____.
                                                          (name of society)

_____   _____
(Owner's signature)   (Date)

Step 4
Advertising the Business

In preparation for the grand opening of their businesses, encourage students to advertise. There are several forms of advertising they can use, depending on the grade level. The following list describes them in levels from easiest to hardest.

1. **Advertisement card**. These are simple 5" x 8" inch cards that students design to advertise their business. They can be posted on a bulletin board or cupboards. They can be colorful and illustrated, and they should have the following information on it: name of business, product(s), business address, prices, and a slogan.

2. **Posters and banners**. Students can design posters or banners that advertise their business. This is a nice art project. You may need to restrict the maximum size. Let students post the posters or banners for a small fee. You may need to set aside a bulletin board for your society's activities. I reserve a whole wall!

3. **Business cards**. Print Shop Deluxe Companion has a great computer program for designing business cards. With a color printer, students can create some really neat cards. Our librarian opened a business to print the students' business cards. The students enjoyed collecting everyone's cards and passing them out to newcomers. It's a great form of advertising.

Sample business cards:

4. **Commercials**. I've had a lot of fun with this one. Have the students write commercials (3 minutes maximum) to advertise their products. Let them hire actors and actresses to practice and perform the commercials. They can then choose to have their commercial videotaped or sign up to have it produced live during *Prime Time*. Use the Prime Time form (page 68).

   Foster creativity by encouraging students to use props, sound effects, and costumes.

   If other classrooms are involved in a Mini-Society, have each class perform commercials for the other.

   Design studies that compare businesses that don't advertise very much with businesses that do.

   Be open-minded to the many different modalities of advertising that the students may want to use.

5. **Directory of Commerce**. I had an ambitious parent prepare a "Directory of Commerce" for another teacher's society. They used it for advertisement before coming to our "Mini-Faire."

Prime Time

Name _____

Address _____

_____

Name of business _____

Name of commercial _____

Length of commercial _____

Actors/Actresses _____

_____

I _____ would like to request my commercial

be aired on _____ _____ at _____ .
              (day)   (date)   (time)

Respectfully submitted,

_____

Owner

From *The Mini-Society Workbook.* © 1996. Teacher Ideas Press. (800) 237-6124.

Step 5
The First Business Day

After students have received their business licenses, designate a day for businesses to operate. Thursdays or Fridays usually work best. At first, not all students will have businesses. Be ready to suggest ideas to students who are struggling with getting a business started. I usually open a business so I have some spending money, too!

Allow 35 minutes for students to conduct business. Here are some helpful hints for a successful business day.

1. Have students set up signs advertising their businesses on colored construction paper (use the society's colors). This makes businesses visible to shoppers.

2. Remind students to display their Business License and address on their desk.

3. Allow 35 minutes, scheduled as follows:
   5 minutes to set up. (*No one* is allowed to shop yet. This includes saving merchandise for a friend!)
   5 minutes for merchants or guests to shop first. When students are busy running their shops, it's hard for them to shop. Letting them shop first rewards those who have put the effort into starting a business.
   20 minutes for everyone (the public) to shop. Many times, a student will ask another student to watch the business. This is fine. Merchants can even hire students to run their stores.
   5 minutes to clean up.

   Note: I have never had problems with students taking other student's things. This program fosters great pride and respect!

Let parents, office staff, grandparents, and relatives get involved as much as possible. They may open a business too! This will generate additional enthusiasm. Periodically invite special guests (the principal, district office staff, and others). Let the class invite guests, too!

Kids get very excited. Remind them to be courteous and to form lines at the businesses.

Always allow time for students to get their ledgers caught up and for discussion afterwards. Discussion helps students identify the economic concepts at work in the Mini-Society.

Step 6
Business Regulations

Food businesses are very successful, but they don't always require the creativity that I find generates pride in the society. If you find food dominating the business industry, here is a suggestion that reduces the food market.

I form an organization like the Food and Drug Administration that regulates all the food businesses. Ask for five volunteers to be on the committee. The society may decide to make the food inspectors government employees. Work with this committee to set some guidelines and restrictions on food businesses. Have the committee make up a name for themselves. They can create badges and other official insignia or documents.

Here is what the Mini-Society called Castle Rock Investigators developed. You may use some of its rules to help your committee get started.

C. R. I. Regulations

1. All food businesses must submit a C. R. I. Nutrition Form and receive C. R. I. approval before opening.

2. All ingredients and labels from food products must be attached to the form.

3. All cans must be recycled.

4. C. R. I. food regulations must be observed. (See lists of approved and disapproved foods.)

5. C. R. I. can close a business that is not in compliance with regulations.

The C. R. I. Nutrition Form and lists of approved foods appear on pages 71-72.

C. R. I. Nutrition Form

Name _____

Name of business _____

Food items sold _____

_____

If an item for sale is bought, attach the container with the ingredients listed.

If an item is homemade, attach the recipe that includes the ingredients and how the item is made (baked, microwaved, or other).

****No substitutions are allowed without C. R. I. approval!****

———————————— Do not write below this line. C. R. I. use only. ————————

Date of approval _____

Initials of committee members _____

If not approved, state reason _____

_____

Dates business was inspected _____

_____

C. R. I. Approved Foods

bottled water
dried fruit processed without sugar
lite (reduced-fat) cheese
lite (reduced-fat) popcorn
nuts without shells
reduced-sodium corn nuts (plain)
string cheese
sugar-free frozen juice bars or fudge bars
sugar-free Kool-Aid
sugar-free pudding with nonfat milk
sugar-free Snow Cones
sugar-free soda
vegetables
washed fruit
whole wheat, sugar-free muffins or breads
whole-wheat crackers

Disapproved Foods

candy
chips
cookies or brownies
gum
ice cream
items in glass containers

junk food or fast food
pizza or hot dogs
snacks with sugar in them
soda and sugar drinks
sunflower seeds with shells

Step 7
Expanding Learning from the Businesses

There are many concepts students can learn by running a business. Don't forget to include in your discussions:

1. Why they sold all of their product.

2. Why they didn't sell all of their product.

3. How fast are they selling? Why?

4. How could they avoid running out of a product?

5. Competition between like businesses and what it does for the consumer and merchant.

6. Is their business experiencing a profit or loss?

7. Why did they close or change businesses?

8. Is it profitable to change products?

9. Is it profitable to have several businesses at the same time?

Help facilitate students' move toward marketing strategies like clearance sales, discounts for visitors (great use of the calculator and using percentages), improvement of product, or gimmicks. (One girl put a special paper in one of her popcorn bags. Whoever bought that bag received a free bag of popcorn.)

If your society doesn't use a checking system, some students may want to establish banks. You'll need to assist them. The one problem I ran into was that whoever set up the bank soon discovered that there was no way to make it profitable. I solved this by allowing them to invest in a simple model of the stock market. Make a dice with the sides marked +0%, +10%, +25%, +50%, +75%, and +100%. Bankers select an amount they want to invest. You can pay dividends out of the class treasury. You may want to set a limit on the amount bankers can invest so the treasury doesn't go broke! Once a week, designate a time that the owners of the banks can tell you how much they are investing. Roll the dice and help them figure out their dividends. Now they have a chance to earn money to pay themselves and their investors.

Provide resource books for your societies. I had one society research courthouses and the judicial system. They set up a court system. Students hired judges, lawyers, defendants, bailiffs, and other officers of the court. They conducted court cases. It was quite fascinating and profitable.

Phase IV
On the Auction Floor

While the businesses are flourishing, introduce the auction concept to generate additional enthusiasm.

The auction concept is a great way for students to generate additional income. The items can be white elephant (someone's junk is another's treasures), items from their businesses (to reduce their inventory before introducing a new product), or purchased items (goldfish, kites, and so forth). The more appealing the items, the more exciting the auction.

If you are the only teacher at your school involved in a Mini-Society, the auction is an easy way to invite other classes to participate in your society. Toward the end of the year, invite another class to auction items in your classroom. (By this time, your own students will be running out of auction items themselves.) The visitors can use the money they earn from their auction at your society's next business day!

A grand auction is an excellent way to end the year. (See phase VI, Culminating the Society.)

Step 1
Preparing for the Auction

1. **Notify the parents.** I have found it very important to once again communicate with parents. Students will be auctioning off their belongings, and you want to make sure it is okay with their parents. To eliminate any problems, send home the It's Auction Time notice (page 78) and the Auction Permission Slip in appendix D.

2. **Designate a day for auctions.** I rotate business days with auctions so that we have one or the other every week. After the first few auctions, you should only need 20 minutes to run one.

3. **Select 6-8 students to sell at each auction.** I place all the students' identification numbers in a jar and have the Auction Officials randomly pick the numbers. I allow students whose numbers are drawn the option to auction or not. Students who commit to sell at an auction and don't participate are fined.

4. **Make sure Auction Officials send home an Auction Permission Slip with each participating student.** Sellers must return the forms on or before auction day to participate. The only time I make an exception is after a personal conversation with the seller's parent.

5. **Make Auction Cards.** A blank 5" x 8" inch card is sufficient. Write each student's number on the upper half of the card, and stamp the card with the society's stamp. Students must have an auction card to participate.

6. **Train Auction Officials and Auction Secretaries.** See phase II, step 6, for detailed instructions.

7. **Rules and Regulations.** Write on the overhead or make a poster of auction rules. Students in grades 7-9 may write the rules and design the poster as a class project.

Here is a sample poster of auction rules:

Auction Rules

1. Once the auction official says, "Quiet on the auction floor," only the auctioneer, seller, secretary, or official may speak.

2. If you talk, your card will be taken for the rest of that auction.

3. If you are willing to pay the spoken price, hold your card up with a straight arm. (*This is to be sure the auctioneer sees it.*)

4. If you buy an item, take the money to the Auction Secretary and pick up the item.

5. If you have hired an auctioneer, be sure the auctioneer has all the sale items *before* the auction begins.

6. Never commit yourself to a price unless you can pay for it.

It's Auction Time!

To the parents of _____ .

    We are progessing nicely here at _____

(name of Mini-Society)

and are ready to start having auctions. If you child's number is chosen, he or she may bring an auction item to school. The item can be an unwanted toy or object, something from the student's business, or even something purchased, although that is not necessary.

    When your child is chosen to sell at an auction, you will need to sign the Auction Permission Slip so I will know it's okay for your child to auction the item. I wouldn't want you to lose a priceless heirloom!

    Thank you for your support.

    Sincerely,

— — — — — — — — — — — — tear off and return — — — — — — — — — — — —

I read your note concerning the auction and understand that I will be responsible

for signing _____'s

(child's name)
permission slip when she/he wants to auction.

Sincerely,

_____

(signature)

Step 2
Quiet on the Auction Floor!

Let the auction (action) begin! The first time you have an auction, you will need to model how an auctioneer talks. Practice at home first!

> Who'll give me
> Ten, ten, ten, ten, ten . . .
> Who'll give me
> fifteen, fifteen, fifteen . . .
> twenty for this beautiful . . .
> twenty, twenty, do I hear
> twenty-five, twenty-five . . .
> . . . going once, going twice,
> SOLD to number 17!

Students will quickly become proficient auctioneers, and students will hire their favorite auctioneers. After the first two auctions, you should be able to sit back and watch (or participate).

Parents really like to see this process. Be sure to let them visit at auction time.

To generate additional enthusiasm, designate an auction day when parents, office staff, and even the principal can auction items. Don't forget that you can auction too. You *will* need the money!

Phase V
Maintaining the Society

By this phase, your society has been fully functioning for some time. If you are reading this book straight through, you might be feeling overwhelmed. Don't! The process is very easy, and the society actually runs itself in a very short amount of time.

Allow the society to expand and develop along with the abilities of your students. Be flexible and seize all learning opportunities as they occur. Don't be afraid to use economic terms (for example, saturation of the market, quality and cost control). Stress the importance of engaging in legal sales. Students can't buy something and resell it unless they have a license to do so. You need to be aware of what is going on so that real money doesn't enter the scene.

As the society grows in complexity, you'll find it will run itself. You'll notice a real sense of unity and pride evolving in the classroom.

Keep all memories in an envelope. This envelope becomes the society's historical archive. Students like to come back and reminisce about good old times. Some classes want to have reunions!

Make a time line of events as they occur.

Send out invitations for guests to visit and participate. It keeps the students motivated.

Don't limit yourself to the classroom. This concept can be expanded by involving other classrooms and schools. I coordinate a Mini-Faire every year, inviting 15 other societies to join us.

If you get other teachers excited, the options are limitless:

passports and visas (appendix E)

Mini-Faire (appendix F)

money exchange/international trade

telecommunicating with other societies

field trips to other societies

sending artifacts to other societies

trying to understand the uniqueness of other societies by examining
their artifacts

participating in government activities

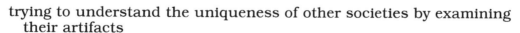

Phase VI
Culminating the Mini-Society

You've made it to the final phase! Students have grown a lot. I find that when I am at this point, it is hard to let go and say goodbye.

Culminating the society is just as important as beginning the society. Make it special. Here are some ideas I've tried that have added to the culmination experience:

1. **Fly the flags.** Hang all previous societies' flags. Share each flag's pledges and history. We have a lot of fun comparing our flags and pledges to those of previous societies.

2. **Final business day.** Encourage the students to make their last business day outstanding. I usually make the Mini-Faire our final full business day, and then have a clearance business day afterward. (See appendix F for complete instructions for setting up a Mini-Faire.)

3. **Final payday.** The last payday is usually the week before school is out, because the last week usually gets pretty crazy!

4. **Grand auction.** Students will begin to realize that after the last day of school their money will have no value. Throughout the last week of school, have a grand auction where all students or parents can auction items—as many as they want! I go to local merchants for certificates and sometimes ask parents to donate auction items. Save a few of the top items for the last day of school. Run the grand auctions without secretaries; it will make them go a lot faster.

5. **Scrapbooks.** One year for the society Astara, one of my very creative and ambitious parents developed a scrapbook for each of the Astarians. The pages were stapled into a folder and personalized with each student's name. It was a great success. (Appendix G offers instructions for this project.)

6. **Culminating party.** Arrange for a special cake with the flag on it and other refreshments. I make this a serious and special time. We take down the flag, and everyone signs either the back of it or a ribbon that is later attached to the flag. We gather around the cake with the flag in hand to say the pledge for the last time. Pictures are taken, videotaping is completed, all artifacts are put in the archive envelope, and the society comes to an end, becoming a part of *history*!

Appendix A:
Classroom Examples

Integrating the Mini-Society concept into your existing social studies curriculum is not only easy, but rewarding and fun. This appendix describes what I did with a fifth-grade class that formed a Mini-Society called Hammertown.

From the following parent update to the final war update, you can see the integration of the social studies curriculum with a Mini-Society.

A New Colony Is Founded . . .

By now you have heard that our ships have landed and L-2 is the colony of Hammertown. We landed on September 7 at 12:11 p.m. The Chiselettes and Road Warriors have formed groups called Chainsaws, Hard Hats, Chisel Heads, Screwdrivers, Silver Bullets, and Slammers. They have designed their currency, called bolts, with the official colony colors of red and black. Employment lines weren't too bad, and government and civilian jobs have been secured. Training is in process.

We are studying the early American colonies and comparing them to our colony. One of the things we discovered was that the Spanish, French, Dutch, and English colonists came to the New World for wealth. That is why we ventured forth, too!

I am looking forward to the many exciting opportunities I have planned for this year.

On behalf of the colony of Hammertown, here's to a great year of learning!

Master Architect Fletcher

As the class learned about the American colonies and the colonists' arrival in the New World, we were developing our colony. Cooking was integrated with the making of Irish soda bread, which was brought to New England in the 1800s by Irish immigrants. Groups competed to create a Hammertown recipe based on our shared heritage.

Cooperative learning groups made posters illustrating the Townsend Act of 1767 and the other taxes and restrictions that were imposed on the colonists. While they were learning this, I got our principal and office staff in on the action, and they began imposing taxes on us! Notice the historical progression that takes place in the notices of new or increased taxes.

Proclamation

To the Colony of Hammertown from the Cedargrove Office:

Due to the poverty level of the office, we must impose a tax on the Colony of Hammertown for the cleaning of your classroom. The tax leveled against you shall be 30 bolts.

Dated: January 16, 1991

His Highness The King

Proclamation

To the Colony of Hammertown from the Cedargrove Office:

Due to the poverty level of the office, we must impose a tax on the Colony of Hammertown for each desk in your classroom. The tax leveled against you shall be three bolts per desk.

Dated: February 1, 1991

His Highness The King

Proclamation

Let it be known that the residents of Hammertown shall pay a tax of two bolts each for library improvements.
Said taxes are due and payable now.

So signed,
The Governess of
Printed Material

Mrs. Sandy McPheron

Proclamation

To the Colony of Hammertown from the Cedargrove Office:

Due to the poverty level of the office, we must impose a tax on the Colony of Hammertown for all the pencils exported to you. The tax leveled against you shall be two bolts per pencil. We have issued you 120 pencils to date this year.

His Highness The King

At this point, the students started peaceful rebellions similar to the American colonists. They marched around the school with signs that said, "No More Taxes" and "Down with Taxes, We're Going Broke."

Working secretly with the principal, I had him make the taxes steeper and steeper to try to create historical unrest and a feeling of wanting their independence. It worked! They formed their first Congress of Hammertown and wrote a letter of protest to the principal, His Highness the King. Here was his response:

Proclamation

To: All residents of the Kingdom
From: His Highness, The King

All subjects must pay an additional tax of two bolts.

In answer to the letters I have received from the residents of Hammertown, I'm sure that you will understand that it costs a great deal of money to support our government, our post office, and our army. It has also been very expensive to enlarge my castle and to pay for my many servants and my many royal parties and sporting events here at the castle. As loyal subjects of the kingdom, I'm sure you will want to work even harder to pay the additional taxes now required.

Dated: This 12th day of February, 1991

As planned, this did not go over well at all. I kept guiding students through history lessons. What did the colonists do? How did they react? A convention was held in April to write the Hammertown constitution. I had the students study the U.S. Constitution and model theirs after it. The class wrote a declaration, everyone signed it, and the class sent it to the King.

The Declaration of Independence

In Congress, March 4, 1991
1:35 p.m.

The unanimous declaration of the colony of Hammertown

When it becomes necessary for separation, because we have respect for you the King, we feel we should let you know why we want separation.

This is what we believe:

All Hammertowners are created equal and have the right to life, freedom, and happiness. The government is designed to protect these rights. When the government no longer protects us, a new government needs to be chosen.

The King has taken our freedom and happiness and has not respected our rights. To prove this, let these facts be submitted to other societies:

He has imposed taxes on us without our consent.

He has used our money to improve his castle, post office, servants, and army.

He has used our money to support his royal parties and sporting events, which did not benefit us.

He has ignored our letters to abolish taxes and has continued to tax us.

He has combined with others in his office (the library, for example) to add additional stress on us.

He has caused a depression to our colony.

He has taxed our colony unfairly and not other societies.

In every phase of taxes we have petitioned for freedom in the most humble terms only to get more taxes. We have protested for our freedom and reminded the King of our needs. We have tried to communicate with him but he has not listened.

We, therefore, the representatives of the Colony of Hammertown, in General Congress assembled, appealing to His Highness, the King, do, in the name and by the authority of the good people of the colony, solemnly publish and declare, that the Hammertown colony is, and of right ought to be, a FREE AND INDEPENDENT STATE!

We shall be absolved from all allegiance to His Highness the King and all political connections will be totally dissolved and as a free and independent state, we have full power to make our own laws, taxes, government, and do all other acts and things that independent states may do. And for the support of this declaration, we mutually pledge to each other that we will work and sweat for our freedom and our sacred honor.

Of course, as history would have it, he didn't respond and war was just around the corner. Following are two newspaper articles written by two students at that time:

The war is about to begin. Hi, I'm Aaron Asuncion. I'm in L-2 and I, at this moment, am writing an article about what we're doing in our colony. Right now we're having problems with taxes. We think we're getting taxed too much (like the early colonists!). A week ago we wrote a Declaration of Independence. We sent it to the King (His Royal Highness Mr. Klinkhart). He didn't accept. He doesn't want us to have our independence. We said we are willing to fight for it. We're going to war on April 19, 1991. I'm looking forward to it. I want us to become a state. Our classroom is going to win. Gooooooo L-2.

The classroom war update by Alicia Franco

Ever since Hammertown became a colony there was a problem, a problem about taxes. Sure we don't like them but either way we have to pay them. Lately Hammertown has been getting a lot of taxes from the King (Mr. Klinkhart). In our last tax we had to pay as usual. Some people were broke. He did respond but did not stop the taxes. The Congress and citizens of Hammertown decided to write a Declaration of Independence and go to war with the King if necessary. So far the war is going to be a race.

Maybe the next time you hear from us we will be the <u>State</u> of Hammertown!

Because our principal is a runner, the class drafted an army of volunteers to race him in our school jog-a-thon. He was a good sport and let us win our independence so we could follow history and become a state. Hammertown made a list of Veterans of the 1992 War of Independence. They got special privileges for fighting for freedom.

Please note that this was done with a group of regular fifth-grade students.

Appendix B:
Government Job Descriptions

ATM Teller Job Description

Time Needed
Varies daily with citizens' needs. Usually won't exceed 15 minutes a day.

Brief Description
Cash citizens' paychecks and personal checks as needed.

Major Responsibilities
1. Set up a cash box and keep a transactions book for it.

2. Be available to cash paychecks and personal checks at citizens' convenience during ATM hours of operation. (Hours may be limited.)

3. Assume responsibility for the cash box.

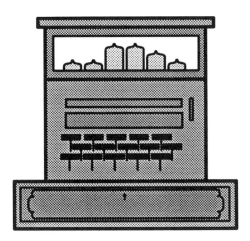

From *The Mini-Society Workbook.* © 1996. Teacher Ideas Press. (800) 237-6124.

Auction Official Job Description

Time Needed
5 minutes to set up and 20-25 minutes to run the auction. Occurs every other week.

Brief Description
Coordinate the auction and keep it running smoothly.

Major Responsibilities
1. Draw numbers to see who will auction every other week.

2. Record all the information for the auction. This includes assigning the Auction Secretaries and Auctioneers.

3. Collect the Auction Permission Slips (page 114) from all the sellers before the auction.

4. Keep the auction running smoothly by calling out who is next to auction. Keep order during the auction.

5. Set up who will auction for the next auction.

Auction Secretary Job Description

Time Needed

25-30 minutes or the duration of each auction.

Brief Description

Record sales information for the auction.

Major Responsibilities

1. Record the auction information in the Auction Secretary's log.

2. Keep track of what is sold and the price paid.

3. Take the money for the item from the buyer and give the money to the seller.

4. Give the sold item to the buyer.

5. Keep records neat and accurate.

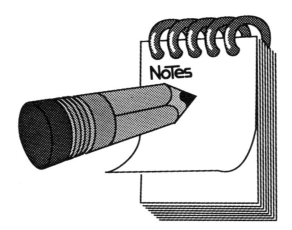

Bank President Job Description

Time Needed
5-10 minutes daily, plus 15 minutes every two weeks.

Brief Description
Responsible for printing each citizen's bank statement every other week. Supervise and assist the Bank Tellers and Operation Manager as needed.

Major Responsibilities
1. Each day, check the Bank Tellers' In boxes to make sure the tellers are caught up.

2. File all the transactions from the Bank Tellers' Out box in the bank transaction file box according to the citizen's individual number.

3. Set up the computer to run each citizen's bank statement every two weeks.

4. Staple each citizen's canceled checks or paychecks to the bank statements and deliver them to each citizen.

5. Help Bank Tellers and the Operations Manager as needed.

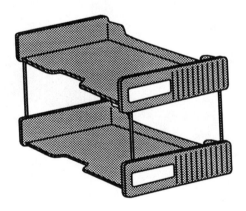

Bank Teller Job Description

Time Needed
10-15 minutes daily.

Brief Description
Enter all bank transactions in the computer for your assigned day.

Major Responsibilities
1. Each day, check your assigned In box for any work to be done.

2. Make sure the checks are endorsed properly and deposit slips are filled out correctly. (For deposits, check to see that the amount of money or the value of the check matches the amount written on the deposit slip.)

3. Each day, enter the transactions into the computer. Be very careful and accurate.

4. Stamp the back of each check with the Entered stamp and date stamp. Initial each transaction completed.

5. Put the completed transaction in the Out box for the Bank President.

6. Report any problems to the Bank President or Operations Manager.

Money Cutter Job Description

Time Needed
Varies with amount of money to be cut.

Brief Description
Neatly and quickly cut out the society's money.

Major Responsibilities
1. Sign the Money Cutters Contract (page 118) and take responsibility when assigned an amount of money to cut.

2. Neatly cut out the money within four working days of receiving it.

3. Return cut money to the teacher, Treasurer, or ATM Teller, who will place it in the treasury.

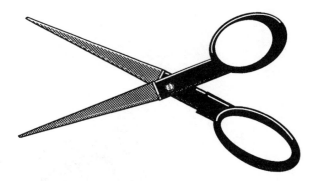

Operations Manager Job Description

Time Needed
10-15 minutes daily. Can vary according to the requests of the Bank President.

Brief Description
Check the Pay Processors' and Bank Tellers' work for accuracy. Assist the Bank President as needed.

Major Responsibilities
1. Before the Pay Processors give their folders to the Treasurers or Payroll Clerks, check folders for accuracy. Use a calculator when needed.

2. Initial all paperwork you review.

3. Assist the Bank President on the day bank statements are run and whenever else you are needed.

Payroll Clerk Job Description

Time Needed
10-15 minutes daily.

Brief Description
Responsible for writing the paychecks and distributing them to the Pay Processors.

Major Responsibilities
1. Make sure the Paycheck Box always has sufficient blank paychecks.

2. Request that more paychecks be printed when the supply is low.

3. Keep a ledger of each paycheck written.

4. Write paychecks based on information received from the Pay Processors on assigned paydays.

5. Put paychecks in the Pay Processor's folder and return the folder to the Pay Processor.

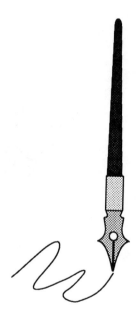

From *The Mini-Society Workbook.* © 1996. Teacher Ideas Press. (800) 237-6124.

Pay Processor Job Description

Time Needed
10-15 minutes daily.

Brief Description
Keep track of each assigned citizen's pay for the week.

Major Responsibilities
1. Set up Pay Processor Sheets (page 120) each week.

2. Each day, record each citizen's salary.

3. Compute each citizen's total weekly salary. On your designated payday, submit to the Treasurer or Payroll Clerk a Pay Processor Sheet for each assigned citizen.

4. Pick up salaries from the Treasurer or Payroll Clerk and pay each citizen. If they are absent, it is your responsibility to pay them when they return. Don't leave the paycheck on their desk.

5. Get new Pay Processor Sheets when needed.

6. *Be very accurate—use a calculator!*

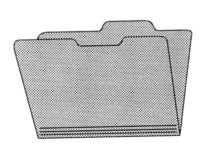
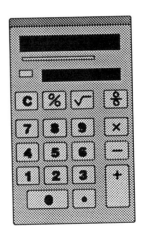

Treasurer Job Description

Time Needed
10-15 minutes daily.

Brief Description
Keep track of all the government monies and distribute salaries to the Pay Processors.

Major Responsibilities

1. Keep the treasury organized. Keep the money neat and in order. Always lock the box containing the treasury's money.

2. Keep the Treasury Book balanced. Use a calculator to figure all deposits and withdrawals. Enter each transaction in the Treasury Book.

3. Check each Pay Processor Sheet for accuracy. Initial the sheets.

4. Place each citizen's pay in the Pay Processor's folder. Stamp with the date and paid stamps.

5. Enter total amount taken out of the treasury, and record the date in the Treasury Book.

6. Lock the treasury box, put it away, and clean up the work area.

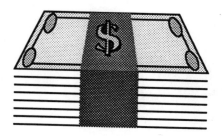

From *The Mini-Society Workbook.* © 1996. Teacher Ideas Press. (800) 237-6124.

Appendix C:
Government Job Applications

ATM Teller Job Application

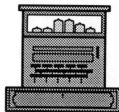

(Please print clearly)

Name _____ Date _____

Address _____

From what you have learned about an ATM Teller, briefly describe the responsibilities.

_____

_____

Why do you think you are qualified for this job? _____

_____

What do you think you will need to learn to become a good ATM Teller?

_____

Why would you like to be an ATM Teller? _____

When students come to you to cash a check or paycheck, what will you look for?

_____

How will you keep track of all the transactions you do each day?

_____

_____

At the end of each day you will need to turn in all the checks you cashed. You will stamp the back of each check. Who processes the checks after this?

_____

What will you use to make sure you are accurate? _____

Who will you go to if you need more money? _____

_____

Auction Official Job Application

(Please print clearly)

Name _____ Date _____

Address _____

From what you have learned about an Auction Official, briefly describe the responsibilities.

_____

_____

Why do you think you are qualified for this job? _____

_____

Why would you like to be an Auction Official? _____

Are you responsible? _____ Are you a good listener? _____

Tell me two things you learned today from listening. _____

_____

_____

Do you have a loud voice? _____ Have you ever made a chart of

something? _____ If so, what? _____

Do you like to find out information from other students? _____

_____

If you get this job, what will you need to find out from those who want to sell items

at an auction? _____

_____

_____

_____

_____

Auction Secretary Job Application

(Please print clearly)

Name _____ Date _____

Address _____

From what you have learned about an Auction Secretary, briefly describe the responsibilities. _____

_____

Why do you think you are qualified for this job? _____

_____

Why would you like to be an Auction Secretary? _____

Are you responsible? _____ Are you a good listener? _____

Tell me two things you learned today from listening. _____

_____

_____

Print "The quick brown fox jumps over the lazy dog."

_____

If Dinky bought an item from an auction for $53.00 and he gave you $60.00, how much would you give him back? _____

_____

From *The Mini-Society Workbook.* © 1996. Teacher Ideas Press. (800) 237-6124.

Bank President Job Application

(Please print clearly)

Name _____ Date _____

Address _____

From what you have learned about a Bank President, briefly describe the responsibilities.

_____

_____

Why do you think you are qualified for this job? _____

_____

What do you think you will need to learn to become a good Bank President?

_____

Why would you like to be a Bank President? _____

In this classroom, how many statements will you have to print every other week?

_____

To whom will you give those statements? _____

Will you attach all the canceled checks to the statements? _____

Who will help you if you need it? _____

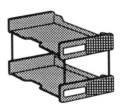

From *The Mini-Society Workbook*. © 1996. Teacher Ideas Press. (800) 237-6124.

 # Bank Teller Job Application

(Please print clearly)

Name _____ Date _____

Address _____

From what you have learned about a Bank Teller, briefly describe the responsibilities.

_____

_____

Why do you think you are qualified for this job? _____

_____

What do you think you will need to learn to become a good Bank Teller?

_____

Why would you like to be a Bank Teller? _____

Do you like working with computers? _____

Who will check your work? _____

How will you check to make sure you have entered all the information into the computer correctly? _____

_____

_____

When will be the best time for you to work on the computer?

_____

From *The Mini-Society Workbook.* © 1996. Teacher Ideas Press. (800) 237-6124.

General Job Application

(Please print clearly)

Name _____ Date _____

Address _____

Which job(s) are you applying for (list in order of preference):

1. _____

2. _____

3. _____

List all other jobs you have had in other classrooms:

_____

_____

_____

Give two references (teacher, friends, parents) who could tell me what kind of worker you are. After their name, write their job title or relationship to you (teacher, principal, friend). Write their phone number if you know it.

1. _____

2. _____

(You may attach letters of recommendation or a copy of your report card from last year.)

From *The Mini-Society Workbook.* © 1996. Teacher Ideas Press. (800) 237-6124.

 # Money Cutter Job Application

(Please print clearly)

Name _____ Date _____

Address _____

From what you have learned about a Money Cutter, briefly describe the responsibilities.

_____

_____

Why do you think you are qualified for this job? _____

_____

Why would you like to be a Money Cutter? _____

Are you responsible? _____ Are you honest? _____

Use a pair of scissors and quickly and carefully cut out these rectangles and staple them to this application.

Operations Manager Job Application

(Please print clearly)

Name _____ Date _____

Address _____

From what you have learned about an Operations Manager, briefly describe the responsibilities. _____

_____

Why do you think you are qualified for this job? _____

_____

What do you think you will need to learn to become a good Operations Manager?

_____

Why would you like to be an Operations Manager? _____
Who does the Operations Manager oversee (check their work)?

_____

What will you use to make sure the math calculations are correct?

_____

Who will you help if they need it? _____
How will you check to make sure the Bank Tellers are entering their information correctly into the computer? _____

_____

Use a calculator to solve the following problem:

> In one week, John received $5.00 for his job and $3.00 each for 4 days for doing his homework. He spent $2.00 to get a drink, got his name in the book 3 days ($4.00 each day), and didn't get in trouble 2 days ($2.00 each day). What is his paycheck?

_____

From *The Mini-Society Workbook*. © 1996. Teacher Ideas Press. (800) 237-6124.

Payroll Clerk Job Application

(Please print clearly)

Name _____ Date _____

Address _____

From what you have learned about a Payroll Clerk, briefly describe the responsibilities.

_____

_____

Why do you think you are qualified for this job? _____

_____

What do you think you will need to learn to become a good Payroll Clerk?

_____

Why would you like to be a Payroll Clerk? _____

From whom will you get the information to write paychecks?

_____

To whom will you give the paychecks when you are finished?

_____

How do you write $1.50 out in words? _____

Where will you keep track of each paycheck you write? _____

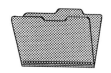 # Pay Processor Job Application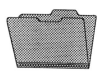

(Please print clearly)

Name _____ Date _____

Address _____

From what you have learned about a Pay Processor, briefly describe the responsibilities.

_____

_____

Why do you think you are qualified for this job? _____

_____

What do you think you will need to learn to become a good Pay Processor?

_____

Why would you like to be a Pay Processor? _____

Whose pay will you be keeping track of? _____

What will you use to make sure you are accurate? _____

How often will you enter information on your record sheets? _____

Use a calculator and the pay scale to solve the following problem:

Sally has a Class B job, did her homework all 4 days, got a drink 1 day, and her name on the board 1 day. What would her paycheck be? _____

Pay Scale	
Reason for Pay or Fine	Amount of Pay or Fine in Sandollars per day
Homework	3
No name on board	3
Name on board	5
No name on paper	-1
Drink	-2
No homework	-6
Bathroom	-10
Reason for pay	Amount in Sandollars per week
Class A job	10
Class B job	7
Class C job	5

From *The Mini-Society Workbook.* © 1996. Teacher Ideas Press. (800) 237-6124.

 # Treasurer Job Application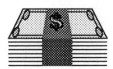

(Please print clearly)

Name _____ Date _____

Address _____

From what you have learned about a Treasurer, briefly describe the responsibilities.

_____

_____

Why do you think you are qualified for this job? _____

_____

Are you a responsible student? _____

Why would you like to be a Treasurer? _____

Use a calculator to solve the following problems:

1. $27.00 + $18.00 + $32.00 + $57.00 + $29.00 = _____

2. $3,032 - $103 = _____

3. If the Money Cutter gave you two $100 bills, five $50 bills, three $20 bills, two $10 bills, two $5 bills, and 20 $1 bills, how much money would you enter into the treasury? _____

4. If you had a balance of $3,664.00 in the treasury and you had to pay a Pay Processor $134.00, what would be the new balance in the treasury?

    _____

From *The Mini-Society Workbook.* © 1996. Teacher Ideas Press. (800) 237-6124.

Appendix D:
Important Documents

Auction Permission Slip

I give _____ my permission to sell
the following at auction:

_____

_____

_____

_____

_____

_____

_____

_____

Sincerely,

_____   _____
(Parent/guardian signature)   (Date)

Bank Statement Reconciliation

1. Look at your bank statement carefully.

2. Subtract any service charges from your checkbook.

3. Sort all your returned (canceled) checks and deposit slips in the order that they appear on your bank statement.

4. Compare each canceled check and deposit slip with your checkbook and bank statement. Check off each that match in both your checkbook and statement.

5. Write your bank statement **ending** balance $_____

6. Add all the deposits that are recorded in your checkbook but don't show up on your statement (that is, deposits that haven't been entered in the computer).

             + _____

7. SUB-TOTAL—ADJUSTED BALANCE   = _____

8. Add all the checks that don't show up on your statement:

   _____ + _____ + _____ +
   _____ + _____ + _____ +
   _____ + _____ = _____

9. Write the total from line 8 on this line.   – _____

10. Subtract line 9 from line 8 to get your NEW BALANCE   _____

    The New Balance should be the same as line 5.

11. Draw a line in your checkbook where it balances and record the date of your statement. Have the teacher review and initial your paperwork.

Checkbook Adjustment Form

Name _____ Date _____

Account # _____

Bank Teller _____

<u>Please list any deposit errors:</u>

Amounts not deposited (staple deposit slips to form for proof)

$ _____ $ _____ $ _____

Amounts deposited twice or incorrectly:

$ _____ $ _____ $ _____

<u>Please list any check withdrawal errors:</u>

Checks not withdrawn that should have been:

Check # _____   Amount $ _____

Check # _____   Amount $ _____

Check # _____   Amount $ _____

Checks that were withdrawn twice or incorrectly:

Check # _____   Amount $ _____

Check # _____   Amount $ _____

Check # _____   Amount $ _____

Attach any paperwork that will be helpful and submit it to the Bank President. The Bank President will initial this form and return it to you after the corrections are made. They will show on your next bank statement.

From *The Mini-Society Workbook.* © 1996. Teacher Ideas Press. (800) 237-6124.

Deposit Slips

Name _____   Deposit Slip

Address _____

_____   _____ 19___

Check # _____   Amount _____

_____

_____

_____

_____

_____

                                    TOTAL DEPOSIT $ _____

Deposit in account # _____

Name _____   Deposit Slip

Address _____

_____   _____ 19___

Check # _____   Amount _____

_____

_____

_____

_____

_____

                                    TOTAL DEPOSIT $ _____

Deposit in account # _____

$Money Cutter's Contract$

I, _____ , certified Money Cutter of

_____ , received and take full
(Society)

responsibility for $ _____ _____
(Total amount)   (Name of currency)

_____ _____
(Witness)   (Date)

_____ _____
(Signature)   (Teacher's signature)

— — — — — — — — — — Job Completion — — — — — — — — — — — —

$ _____ was turned in to the treasury on _____ .
This is the total amount the Money Cutter was given.

_____ _____ _____
(Treasurer's signature)   (Money Cutter's signature)   (Witness)

Paychecks

Name _____   Check #_____

Address _____

_____   Date _____ 19____

PAY TO THE

   ORDER OF _____ $ _____

_____

For _____   _____

Acct # _____

Name _____   Check #_____

Address _____

_____   Date _____ 19____

PAY TO THE

   ORDER OF _____ $ _____

_____

For _____   _____

Acct # _____

Pay Processor Sheet

Name _____ of _____

Address _____

Jobs _____ Salary _____

_____ _____

_____ _____

Subject	Mon.	Tues.	Wed.	Thurs.	Fri.
Homework					
Behavior					
Job					
Job					
Taxes					
Taxes					
Other					
Other					
Daily Totals					

Date paid _____ Grand Total _____ Treasurer's Initials _____

Subject	Mon.	Tues.	Wed.	Thurs.	Fri.
Homework					
Behavior					
Job					
Job					
Taxes					
Taxes					
Other					
Other					
Daily Totals					

Date paid _____ Grand Total _____ Treasurer's Initials _____

Personal Ledger

Name: _____

Date	Description (received from or paid to)	Deposit (+)	Withdrawal (-)	Balance (=)

From *The Mini-Society Workbook.* © 1996. Teacher Ideas Press. (800) 237-6124.

Appendix E:
Tourist Documents

This appendix offers instructions for making a number of documents. Full-size examples are provided.

Passports

To make the sample passport, copy all of the pages, in order, onto both sides of four sheets of paper (figures E-1(a) and E-1(b)) are the front and back of the first sheet of paper, figures E-2(a) and E-2(b) are the front and back of the second sheet of paper, and so forth.) Stack the pages in order, with Figure E-1(a) face down on the bottom of the stack. Fold the stack in half, so that the cover of the passport is on top. Staple along the fold and trim the pages.

If you like, photocopy Figures E-1(a) and E-1(b) onto construction paper and laminate it before assembling the passport. This makes a sturdy cover.

Figure E-1(a). Page 1, front.

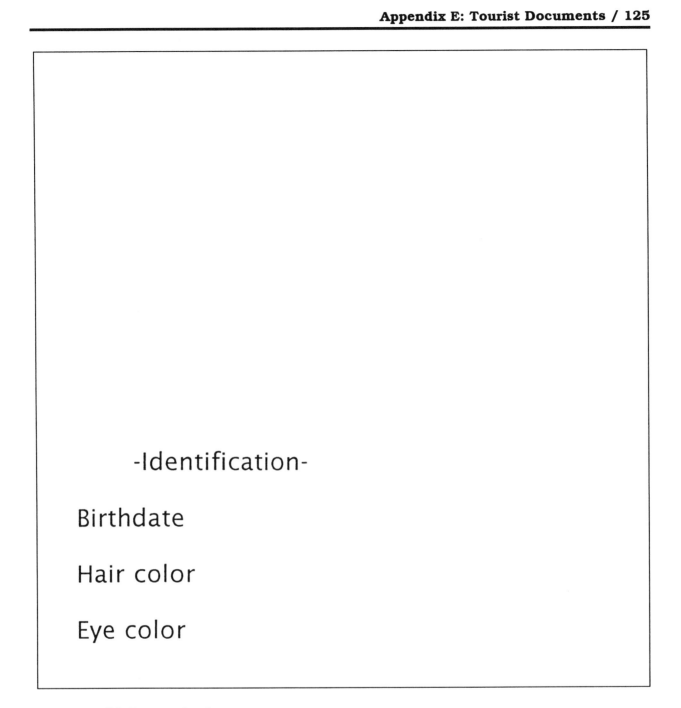

-Identification-

Birthdate

Hair color

Eye color

Figure E-1(b). Page 1, back.

VISA STAMP

Number

Name

Address

𝔗his passport is the
property of 𝔏ost 𝔏agoon

VISA STAMP

Admiral Fletcher

Figure E-2(a). Page 2, front.

VISA STAMP

The Sea Serpents and Flamingos of
Lost Lagoon
request all whom it may concern to
permit the citizens of Lost Lagoon
to pass without delay or
hinderance.

VISA STAMP

Figure E-2(b). Page 2, back.

VISA STAMP

This passport must not be used by any person other than the person to whom it is issued.

VISA STAMP

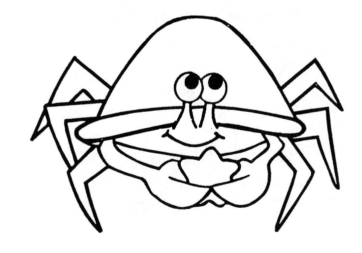

Figure E-3(a). Page 3, front.

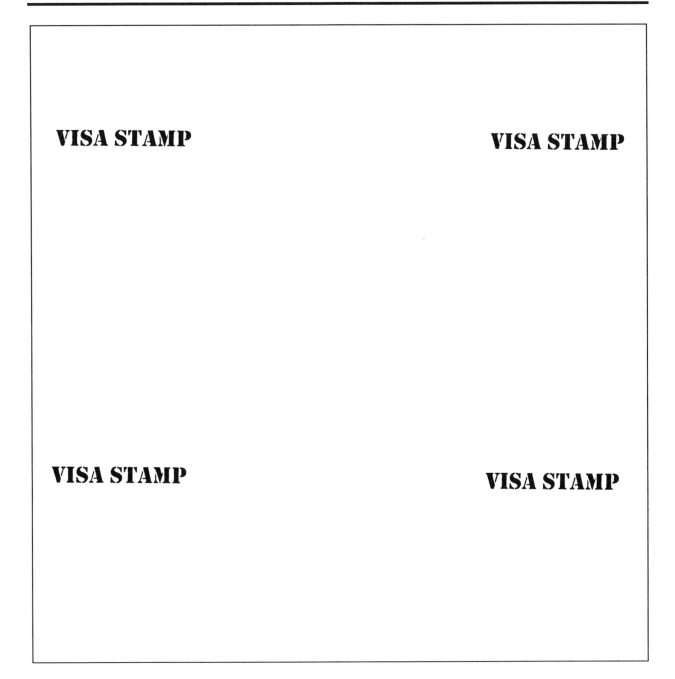

Figure E-3(b). Page 3, back.

VISA STAMP　　　　　　　　　　**VISA STAMP**

VISA STAMP　　　　　　　　　　**VISA STAMP**

Figure E-4(a). Page 4, front.

Figure E-4(b). Page 4, back.

Visas

If citizens want to visit other societies before their passports are finished, make temporary visas on 5" x 8" inch cards. Following is a visa used by the Hammertown Mini-Society. Page 133 includes blank visas you can use in your Mini-Society.

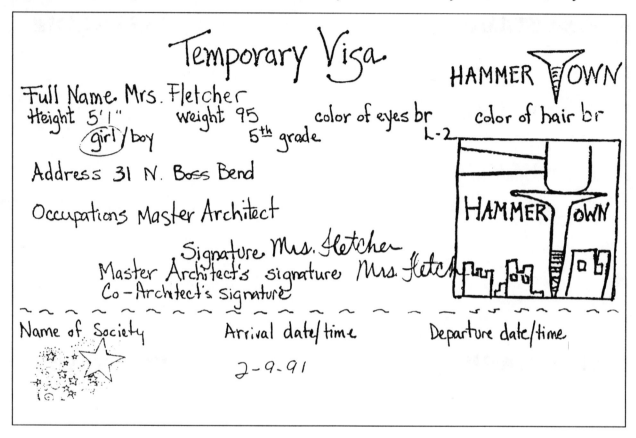

Temporary Visa

Full name: _____   Name of Society _____

Address: _____   Height _____

_____   Weight _____

Occupations: _____   Gender _____

_____   Grade _____   (Society Stamp)

Color of hair _____ Color of eyes _____

Citizen's Signature _____

Authorized Signature 1 _____

Authorized Signature 2 _____

- -

Name of Society   Arrival Date/Time   Departure Date/Time

Temporary Visa

Full name: _____   Name of Society _____

Address: _____   Height _____

_____   Weight _____

Occupations: _____   Gender _____

_____   Grade _____   (Society Stamp)

Color of hair _____ Color of eyes _____

Citizen's Signature _____

Authorized Signature 1 _____

Authorized Signature 2 _____

- -

Name of Society   Arrival Date/Time   Departure Date/Time

V.I.P. Cards

This is a passport I use whenever guests visit the room or come to a Mini-Faire. I usually give visitors some spending money to promote good public relations! Following is a V.I.P. card used by the Lost Lagoon Mini-Society. Page 135 includes blank V.I.P. cards you can use in your Mini-Society.

V.I.P. Passport # _____

_____
Print name and title

_____
Signature

This special government passport issued by LOST LAGOON entitles the bearer to travel to any society free of emigration procedures and restrictions.

Mrs. Fletcher
Admiral of Lost Lagoon

Valid only on May 27, 1994

V.I.P. Passport # _____

_____
Print name and title

_____
Signature

This special government passport issued by _____
entitles the bearer to travel to any society free of emigration procedures and restrictions.

_____
Authorized Signature

Valid only on _____

(Society Stamp)

V.I.P. Passport # _____

_____
Print name and title

_____
Signature

This special government passport issued by _____
entitles the bearer to travel to any society free of emigration procedures and restrictions.

_____
Authorized Signature

Valid only on _____

(Society Stamp)

Appendix F:
Coordinating a Mini-Faire

Mini-Faires are the best way to join others in celebrating your society's development. Coordinating a Mini-Faire is a lot of work. This appendix includes everything you need to produce a successful Mini-Faire. Of course, you'll need other Mini-Societies to invite. You can start out small, with other Mini-Societies at your school. If you can't find any Mini-Societies your first year, contact me and I might be able to help you locate some.

Here are some steps toward making it a reality.

1. **Talk to your principal about a date and facilities.**

2. **Send invitations.** Following is a sample invitation:

Mini-Faire '94 Is Coming Soon!
Are You?????

What is it?

A faire in which 15 societies from different school districts get together for intersociety trade. Merchants set up booths to sell their wares or services. Everyone brings their passports, flags, society currencies, and spirit.

When is it?

Friday, May 27, 9-11 a.m.

Where is it?

Cedargrove Elementary School
1209 N. Glendora Ave.
Covina, CA 91724

How can I be included?

Registration is by invitation only, on a first-come, first-served basis.

Simply fill out the enclosed form, include $5 to cover registration and mailings, and send it to:

Kathleen Fletcher
611 N. Vista Bonita Ave.
Glendora, CA 91741

You will be sent a confirmation slip, entry number for set up, and packet of information to help you prepare for the special day. Please make sure you can come before you register. (If the faire is full by the time I receive your registration, your $5 will be refunded.)

Hope to see you on May 27, 1994!

Sincerely,
Admiral Fletcher
and the Flamingos and Sea Serpents of Lost Lagoon

Following is a sample registration form.

Mini-Faire Registration '94

Teacher _____ Grade _____

School _____ District _____

Address _____

School Phone _____ Home Phone _____

Address to send information _____

_____

Name of society _____

Title of teacher _____

Name of boys _____ Girls _____

Money _____ Colors _____

Special groups _____

_____

_____

Please enclose $5 to cover registration and mailing costs.

Mail registration to:

_____

_____

_____

_____

Following is a sample questionnaire.

Mini-Society Questionnaire

Teacher _____ Grade _____

School _____ Room Number _____

Name of society _____

Title of teacher _____

Name of boys _____ Girls _____

Money _____ Colors _____

Special groups _____

_____

_____

_____

_____

This questionnaire provides information about the visiting Mini-Societies to share with your students and to use for program information.

3. **Confirm reservations.** As responses to the invitations come in, send to each visiting group a confirmation sheet and information about the faire.

Following (on pages 140-41) is a sample confirmation letter and information.

Congratulations!

A spot is reserved for you at Mini-Faire '94, Thursday, May 27.

Your set-up number is _____

Mini-Faire Information

Where: Cedargrove Elementary School
1209 N. Glendora Ave., Covina (818) 966-8765

When to Arrive: 8:30-9:00 a.m.
Teachers: Please check in at the arrival table before you set up.

What to Bring:

- Your **flag** (make sure it is on a dowel).
- A **banner** with the name of your society. This will hang on your money exchange/passport stamping table.
- **2 card tables** for money exchange and stamping passports.
- Several sheets of **12" x 18" inch construction paper** in your society's colors. You will need one sheet for each business. The sheets will be used to cover tables in your merchant's booths.
- **Passports.** Make sure there are several pages for other societies' visa stamps.
- **Visa stamp** to stamp in other societies' passports.
- **Date stamp** to use with visa stamp (optional).
- **Treasury.** Bring plenty of currency in all denominations.
- **Business licenses, ledgers, and calculators** (if needed).
- **Large index cards stating prices** (one or more cards for each business).
- An **envelope** for each business. Shoppers can put their money in them if the merchant is not at the business at the time they purchase something.
- **14 large manila envelopes.** Put a sample of your money on the front of each.
- **Several parents** to stamp passports, exchange money, and help students.

Set-Up Instructions:

Have students set up their businesses on your designated tables (see map).
Hang banner on front of card tables for money and passports.
Encourage students to set up quickly.
When you are finished, have students stand behind their tables. Keep your flag with you.

Students are not to roam around yet!

Flag Ceremony: 9:15 sharp!

After everyone is set up, we will salute the American flag. I will then call each Mini-Society to come forward (one at a time). Come to the stage, led by your flag bearer. Face the audience and recite your pledge. Place your flag in a holder and return to your assigned area.

Special Immigration Rules and Regulations

1. Exchange rate:

    We will do a simple 1-for-1 exchange to make exchanges easier. If a student hands your money changer 10 coral cash "dollars," your money changer will hand the student 10 of your currency.

2. Students will be able to use only the correct currency in each Mini-Society. PTA parents will go to each money exchange table to re-exchange money. As you accumulate coral cash, the PTA parents will re-exchange it back to your currency, so you won't run out. At the end of the fair, have your parents re-exchange the currency.

3. Students will need to get their passport stamped only once at each society.

4. Students may watch each other's businesses. Parents can help run businesses, too. This allows every student to shop.

5. Please encourage all your students to be polite and wait in line. Remind them that we respect others' property and products.

6. When the fair is over, encourage each student to stop shopping, leave the society they are in, and help clean up.

Thank you so much for coming. I am looking forward to a unique and exciting learning experience for all our students.

Sincerely,

Kathleen Fletcher
Captain, Ocean's End

4. **Get everything ready!** This is the hardest step. I have lots of fun making special buttons, banners, and other specialty items for the big event. Make lists of everything you'll need so you don't forget anything in the last-minute rush. Here is a sample list:

Things to Do

Mail invitation packets
Organize responses
Create agenda and schedule for Mini-Faire
Mail instructions
Make passports
Make buttons
Make visa stamp
Request tables, chairs, trash cans, PA system
Make banner for registration table and society
Make or get a vinyl banner for school
Make a map of the Mini-Faire area, with areas assigned to Mini-Societies
Make packets for visiting teachers—welcome, map, agenda, button
Make VIP passports for visitors
Organize parent helpers
Make a clipboard
Write opening speech
Set up tables, chairs, and trash cans
Hang banners
Check PA system
Set up American flag
Set up registration table
Set up our Mini-Society's businesses, exchange table, and passport table
Set up flag holders in middle
Direct other Mini-Societies and help them set up

Things to Have

Tables, chairs, trash cans, PA system
American flag
Flag holders
Extra flag poles, our Mini-Society's flag
My passport and money
Clipboard with society information, speech, map, other important papers
Tape, scissors, pens
Construction paper for businesses
Banners (vinyl, registration, society)
Videocamera and tape, still camera
Visa stamp, stamp pad, date stamp, treasury box with money
Grocery bags for shoppers
Twine to hang banner
Extra envelopes for money
Registration packets—V.I.P. passports, name tags, teacher info, money for guests
My own business stuff

Parent Helpers

One or two parents to run registration (instructions on registration packet).

One parent to stamp passports with visa and date stamp.

Two parents to exchange money for students entering our Mini-Society.

One parent to re-exchange money (This parent will go to each society every 15 minutes and pick up all other societies' money and redistribute it to the society of origin). Parent carries large envelopes to do this.

One parent to videotape bits and pieces of the fair: societies arriving, flag ceremony, shopping.

5. **Prepare a welcome packet for guests.** I include a program that lists all the participating Mini-Societies. I also include a map that shows each Mini-Society's assigned set-up spot.

    Following is a sample program:

Mini-Societies Present Today

Ocean's End	Cedargrove	Charter Oak USD
Sportsmania	Cedargrove	Charter Oak USD
Brandtly Hills	Washington	Charter Oak USD
Cross Vegas	Washington	Charter Oak USD
Rad Village	Stanton	Glendora USD
Diamond Valley	Stanton	Glendora USD
Surfer City	Stanton	Glendora USD
The Surfing Dogs	Merwin	Covina-Valley
Super Coast Cruisers	Wedgeworth	Hacienda-La Puente
Radical Fifth Graders	Wedgeworth	Hacienda-La Puente
California Nerds Society	Wedgeworth	Hacienda-La Puente
Classiety	Dunsmore	Glendale USD
M.E. (Mini-Enviroment)	Dunsmore	Glendale USD
Foreign Exchange students	Cedargrove	Charter Oak USD

A Special Thanks To

A-1 Rentals (tables)

Cedargrove PTA and office staff

Betty Abel (flag holders)

All teachers, parents, administrators, and students who made this faire possible.

Enjoy the Faire!

Captain Fletcher, Colony of Ocean's End

---

6. **Review the To Do, To Have, and Parent Helpers lists.** Create a schedule to do or obtain everything; assign tasks to volunteers; and coordinate completion of all tasks.

7. **The Mini-Faire Day.** Set up a registration table near the entrance to the Mini-Faire-ground. Be sure to hang a large sign on the table, and use signs or greeters at the entrance to direct all visitors to go directly to the registration table.

At the registration table, greet visitors and

a. Check off the school on a master list of visitors.

b. Hand the society's leader a packet containing information and a button inside.

c. Collect their money envelopes. (Place the small ones in the large one.)

d. Issue a V.I.P. passport to guests not associated with a Mini-Society, such as administrators or district office personnel. Also give the V.I.P. guests a V.I.P. name tag.

e. After you register everyone, please distribute one money envelope from each society (a large manila envelope with a sample of the society's money taped on it) to each society. Keep the large ones for the parents who will exchange the money back.

On the big day, just follow your agenda. Following is a sample agenda:

Mini-Faire Agenda

8:30-9:00	Set-up
9:00-9:15	Assemble for the flag ceremony
9:15-9:40	Flag ceremony
9:40-11:00	MINI-FAIRE
11:00-11:20	Clean-up and farewell

---

8. **Sleep in the next day!** You won't be able to though, because you will be so excited about the wonderful experience your students had yesterday!

Appendix G:
Sample Scrapbook

Planet Astara

Discovered: September 1988

Commanded by: Mrs. K. Fletcher

Astarian Flag Salute

Let's set a course for Astara, ahead, warp speed . . .

We pledge loyalty to all Androids and Asteroids and dedicate ourselves to the preservation of our galactic quest. We shall work for progress in all that we do. Lightspeed shall be our goal. We shall seek peace with all life forms of the universe and will always use caution upon entering hyperspace.

Beam us up, Scotty!

From *The Mini-Society Workbook.* © 1996. Teacher Ideas Press. (800) 237-6124.

Class Photo

Job Descriptions

I held the job of: _____

My duties were: _____

My salary was: _____

These are the other five things I will include in my scrapbook:

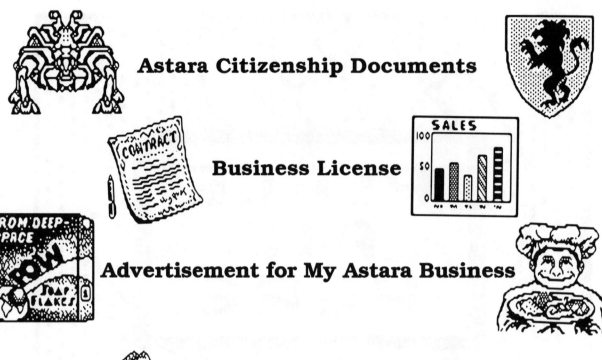

Astara Citizenship Documents

Business License

Advertisement for My Astara Business

Astarian Currency

Autographs of Fellow Astarians

About the Author

Kathleen D. Fletcher

Kathleen Fletcher has been an elementary classroom teacher in Los Angeles USD and Charter Oak USD for the past 16 years. She has conducted numerous workshops and speaking engagements in her Mini-Society program and manipulative mathematic techniques throughout southern California. The last few years she has been working with gifted students in the G.A.T.E. program.

Kathleen is currently on a leave of absence from Charter Oak USD, and is teaching full time in the teacher education program at Azusa Pacific University and working on her Ph.D. in curriculum and instruction.

She is the recipient of several teaching awards, including the 1995-1996 Teacher-of-the-Year award from her elementary school, Mathematics Teacher Nominee of the year from LAUSD, and the Good Apple Award. Her love for teaching is evident in her students' love of learning from the enriching environments she provides.